James Smart of Chalford

Working Life
on the Cotswold Canals
and Linked Waterways

Hugh Conway-Jones

Black Dwarf Publications

A typical Stroud barge under horse tow approaching Chalford Chapel Lock circa 1838. The owner's name appears to be John Knight, who ran the coal wharf later taken over by James Smart.

About the Author

Hugh Conway-Jones is a retired engineer who has been studying the history of Gloucestershire waterways for over forty years. His previous books include *Gloucester Docks – an Illustrated History*, concentrating on the docks and warehouses at Gloucester, *Working Life on Severn & Canal*, describing the life of the boatmen carrying goods through to the Midlands, and *The Gloucester & Sharpness Canal – an Illustrated History*, telling the story of the ship canal to Gloucester.

Contents

Published by BLACK DWARF PUBLICATIONS
© Black Dwarf Publications & Hugh Conway-Jones 2020
Designed by Neil Parkhouse

British Library Cataloguing-in-Publication Data. A catalogue record for this book is available from the British Library
ISBN: 9781903599 29 7

BLACK DWARF LIGHTMOOR PUBLICATIONS LTD
Unit 144B, Lydney Trading Estate, Harbour Road, Lydney, Gloucestershire GL15 4EJ
www.lightmoor.co.uk
Black Dwarf Publications is an imprint of Black Dwarf Lightmoor Publications Ltd

Printed in Poland
www.lfbookservices.co.uk

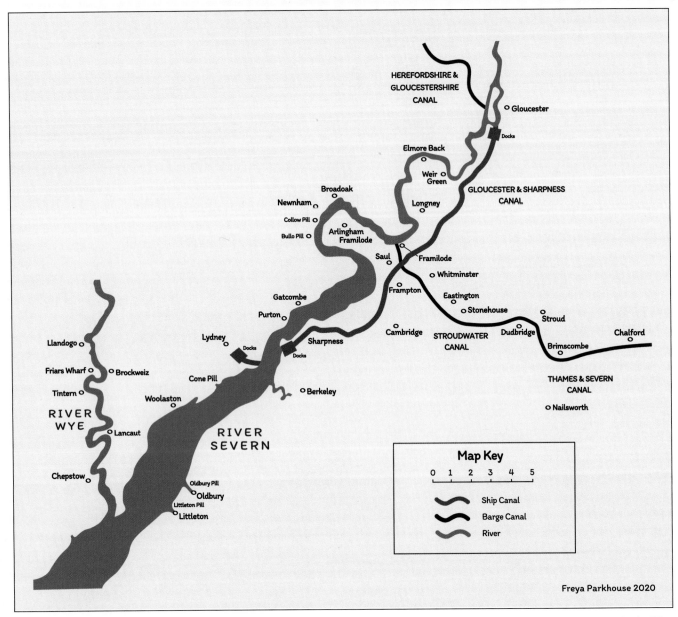

Map of the waterways used by James Smart's boats and barges in Gloucestershire. For waterways in the West Midlands see map on Page 22, and for Wiltshire, Berkshire and Oxfordshire see page 124.

Chapter 1

Setting the Scene

In the 19th century, the Stroudwater and Thames & Severn canals were well used by canal boats and barges, mainly bringing raw materials to the communities along the two waterways and also exporting some local products. Coal was brought in from the Forest of Dean, Staffordshire and South Wales, whilst road stone came from Bristol and Chepstow. Imported grain and timber were carried eastwards, and local grain and timber westwards, with much cut timber being sent to the Midlands. The boats and barges were owned and crewed by local people, and the village of Chalford became a centre for these activities after it had been particularly hit by the decline of the Stroud Valley's woollen cloth industry.

Among those who found work on the canals were two brothers named William and Charles Smart. William's son, James, also joined him in the late 1840s at the age of nine. At that time, William was captain of the narrow boat *Emma*, owned by Edward Restall of Daneway, at the head of the valley above Chalford. Restall ran a saw mill, evidently

Daneway Wharf circa 1908, with the bridge over the Thames & Severn Canal and the Daneway Inn, popular with boatmen, behind. MM

processing timber from local estates and *Emma* regularly carried planks, round timber and sometimes bedsteads to Birmingham, returning with Staffordshire coal. As was common at that time for the son of a bargeman, James never learned to read or write.

In 1851, William and James transferred to the barge *Mary Ann* and later to *Lady Sale*, both owned by coal merchant Joseph Smith of Cirencester, regularly collecting around 35 tons of Forest of Dean coal from Bullo Pill and delivering it to Cirencester. This quantity was less than the capacity of these barges and was presumably determined by the available depth of water on the summit level of the Thames & Severn Canal, where it crossed the high ground of the Cotswolds. When traversing the summit, whilst William worked the barge through Sapperton Tunnel with the help of a hobbler, James rode the towing donkeys over the top of the hill. Part of this route was through woodland and James later recalled how on dark nights he used to put his bare feet up on the donkey's back, for fear the foxes might get at his toes.

In 1855, the barge *Lady Sale* passed into the ownership of coal merchant Samuel Aldum of Chalford, with William and James continuing as crew. A year later they transferred to the barge *Sampson*, owned by Samuel Aldum's son John, based at Wallbridge, Stroud. Under the Aldums' management, better use was made of the capacity of the barges, as they regularly collected around 45 tons of coal from Lydney or Bullo Pill, most being delivered to places along the Stroud Valley but with some part-loads continuing over the summit. Notable destinations included the Canal Company's steam pumping engine at Thames Head, and Radcot and Tadpole Bridge on the River Thames.

On one such trip along the Stroudwater Canal in March 1858, while Sampson was passing through Eastington Lock, William Smart accidentally fell from the side of the lock and was drowned. By this time, James had had nine years' experience of working boats and barges, and his employer thought well enough of him to appoint him captain of *Sampson* and later of *Gem*. With these barges, James continued to carry coal from Lydney and Bullo Pill to places along the Stroud Valley and up into the Cotswolds. Three years after his father died, James Smart married Martha Ann Brown, the daughter of a Chalford carpenter, and the couple were soon raising a family. He worshipped regularly at Christ Church, Chalford, usually sitting in the gallery; when he was away on a trip, he frequently walked from as far away as Saul or Framilode in order to be with his family for Sunday worship. However, following a misunderstanding, he later transferred his loyalty to Chalford Tabernacle.

After ten years working a barge for someone else, in 1869, James Smart went into business on his own account, when he became owner and captain of the barge *Perseverance*, previously owned by coal merchant James Webb of Chalford. Like the other barges he had worked on, this was of the type now known as

James Smart's mark on a memorial from barge owners and others, complaining of the difficulties of navigating the Thames & Severn Canal in 1874. GA D1180/5/15 With permission from the Company of Proprietors of the Stroudwater Navigation

James Smart's barge **Perseverance** *moored adjacent to the works of steam boat builders Abdela & Mitchell, west of Brimscombe. Note the side cloths to protect the cargo and the small mast to which the tow-rope was attached when the main mast was lowered. CoM 1988/164/1*

a Stroud barge, which could pass the full length of both the Stroudwater and Thames & Severn canals. It had a length of 68ft 3ins to suit the locks on the Stroudwater Canal and a breadth of 12ft 6ins to pass through the longer but narrower locks on the Thames & Severn Canal, along with an open hold, a sharp stern and probably a square sail too for use in the estuary. With this vessel, he regularly carried 50-55 tons of coal from Lydney to supply coal merchants along the Stroud Valley as far as Chalford, whilst occasionally also making trips to Bristol. Although unable to read or write, it was said that Smart had excellent business qualities and a wonderful memory, and he was much assisted by his wife who handled the paperwork.

This business was evidently successful as, in 1872, James Smart was able to invest in a second barge, named *Industry* and also previously owned by James Webb. Smart initially became captain of *Industry* but after two years he employed others as captains while he concentrated on developing his business. Another barge was added to the fleet in 1876, when *Flora* was built at Ezra Gardiner's yard at The Bourne, Brimscombe. These two barges had open holds and a single mast like *Perseverance*, although each had a square stern when registered in 1883. They could carry up to 60 tons and mainly traded to Chepstow and ports in the Bristol Channel.

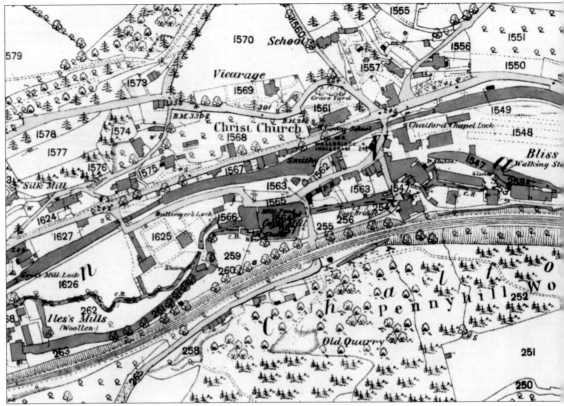

The route of the Thames & Severn Canal through Chalford, as shown on the 1885 1st edition OS. Smart's wharf and house are directly across the canal from Christ Church.

Also in the mid 1870s, James Smart invested in some narrow canal boats, notably *Martha Ann* (named after his wife), *Kate* and *Beatrice* (named after two daughters), and *Civility* and *Charity*. These were particularly used to bring Staffordshire coal to places along the Stroud Valley and also for some more local movements. Smart's brother Jesse worked as a captain on these boats for many years.

Having a fleet of barges and boats, James Smart became well established as a carrier of cargoes for other people, so he decided to take the next step by becoming a merchant himself. In 1879, he took the opportunity of buying the coal wharf, house and out-buildings adjoining the basin at Chalford, previously occupied by the Knight family, part-financed by a mortgage which took thirty years to pay off. From these premises, Smart operated as a coal and brick merchant, bringing in goods by boat and barge, and making local deliveries by horse and cart. His fleet also continued to carry cargoes for other people; notable early examples included coal to Duxford on the River Thames east of Lechlade and to Buscot distillery at Buscot House near Faringdon. A later traffic of boilers and machinery from Buscot to Bowbridge is likely to have been from the distillery when it closed in 1879.

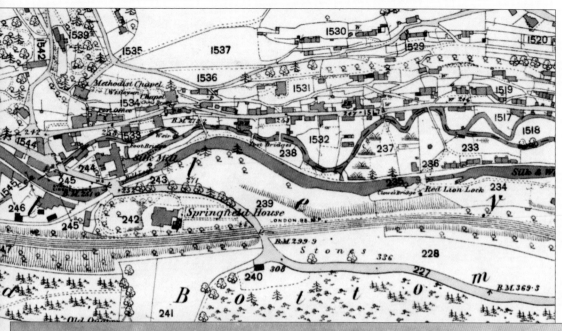

Chalford basin and round house, with James Smart's house in the background. The house, round house and part of the basin survive today. GA D2899

The source material for this book – two examples of the letters to James Smart, from boatmen W. Pearce and J. Davis (BELOW), and Davis on his own (BELOW RIGHT). GA D4848

The way James Smart's business operated over the following years is revealed by a remarkable collection of over 1,000 surviving letters, postcards and telegrams sent to Smart in the 1880s and 1890s by his customers, his suppliers and his boatmen. These show that he traded extensively as far afield as Staffordshire, South Wales, Bristol, the Thames Valley and Wiltshire, and even occasionally to Cheshire, Lancashire and Yorkshire. The following chapters are largely based on these letters, which have been cross-referenced with the corresponding voyages recorded in the tonnage books of the relevant canal companies.

In the letters, James Smart's larger vessels were sometimes referred to as 'barges' and sometimes as 'trows'. In earlier times, the two terms had different meanings but, by the 1880s, the distinction had become blurred, with both terms being applied to a vessel with an open hold and a flat bottom. As the term 'barge' was more widely used in the letters, it will be used in the following chapters. Smart's smaller vessels were usually referred to as 'boats', meaning narrow canal boats, therefore this will be continued. The man in charge of a barge was usually called the 'master' in official documents associated with the Board of Trade but in the letters he was always referred to as the 'captain' and therefore this will also be continued in the following chapters.

Chapter 2

Going Up Country

During the 1880s and 1890s, James Smart of Chalford owned half a dozen narrow canal boats that made regular trips 'up country', to the Midlands to collect coal, often carrying a cargo on the outward journey. Each boat typically made ten to fifteen trips in a year, each lasting two to three weeks.

To crew his boats, James Smart employed men who lived in Chalford. The bylaws for the Stroudwater Canal required three able persons to be on board each vessel, although the Company did not enforce this rule for boats – only for barges. One census return for Smart's boats in the Midlands shows three men on board but usually there were only two, sometimes including a teenage son. Wives usually stayed at home. Before setting out, the boat captain was given some starting money as an advance on his and his crew's wages, and to pay any anticipated canal tolls. On the way, he was expected to keep an account of any freight charges received and any expenses paid out, and everything was settled up when he returned. The men were not paid by the hour but by the trip, so they might be on the move for twelve hours a day or even more to get the job done quickly.

It seems the men were also given some food, as surviving receipts show that James Smart regularly bought meat and potatoes from R. Edwards, who ran the Old Red Lion at Chalford. William Staddon later remembered that, when working with his father, they always had a good food cupboard on board: '*There was plenty of beef, ham, pork or sausages, and I was very fond of spearing pike, which gave a bit of variety. One thing I was always glad to get home for was to have a piece of bread and butter, as my father did not have either cheese or butter on his boat*'. Smart also provided food for the two donkeys or one horse that towed the boat.

As a crew set out, they were given an outline of where they were expected to go but some details were often left to be settled later by correspondence, as shown by the many letters from boatmen to James Smart that have survived. These report such matters as

Painting of Wallbridge Basin by J.N. Bolton, showing a boat under tow probably heading 'up country'. To the left of the basin is the entrance to the Thames & Severn Canal and the gates of the first lock.
M1P 2007.183/1488A

Pike Bridge, Eastington circa 1908, with a barge at the nearby coal wharf and a boat towed by a pair of donkeys, which was probably bound for the Midlands. HB

recent experience, current location and intended action, and they often include requests for instructions and/or for money to be sent urgently as an advance on their wages. The letters provide remarkable insights into the boatman's role in managing the business of the boat; some include information about or requests from other boatmen who were, perhaps, illiterate.

An important factor in sustaining this water-borne traffic in the face of railway competition was that there was a ready supply of cargoes for the boats to carry on their outward journeys. There were several saw mills along the Stroud Valley that converted home-grown timber into planks, staves, poles and other shapes that were sent on to timber merchants, factories and workshops in Birmingham and the Black Country. For firms that had canal-side premises, it was cheaper to receive goods by boat rather than by rail and road, which required additional handling. For James Smart's boats, the principal sources of such cargoes were Ebley and Ryeford saw mills, with some also from Griffin's Mill.

James Smart was occasionally asked to take other goods from the Stroud Valley. Cargoes of round timber included beech from Cirencester to Birmingham and oak from Daneway to Manchester. Manganese ore that had been imported by paint manufacturers S.G. Bailey & Co, of Stafford Mill was sent on to the Potteries district for use as a colouring agent. Flour from Kemble & Dash of Stratford Mills was sent to Worcester but the recipient of one load complained that ten sacks were wet. Some boats left the valley without a cargo but with every expectation that they could load imported timber at Gloucester.

Unfortunately, one trip to Birmingham started badly in February 1884. As the boat *Charity* was approaching Whitminster Lock, steerer Richard Wright somehow fell overboard. His fellow crewman immediately stopped the boat and jumped into the water but Wright had gone out of sight and when the body was found, life was quite extinct. At an inquest at the Whitminster Inn, the jury returned a verdict of accidental death.

If there was no cargo from the Stroud Valley to take to Birmingham, James Smart's boats could usually load timber from merchants based at Gloucester Docks. One letter from Barkworth & Spaldin asked: '*Have you any boats you want loading for up the country? We can give you half a dozen loads at once if you can please send up any*'. An agent for a Cardiff importer wanted eight or nine boats to load for Birmingham and Oldbury, and asked for as many

Timber yards lining the Sharpness Canal to the south of Gloucester in 1892, where Stroudwater boats frequently loaded timber for the Midlands. NMM P4769

as Smart could spare. A letter from Price, Walker & Co. asked for a boat to pick up a part load at Sharpness and the rest at Gloucester, all to be sent on to Birmingham. Having this convenient source of outward cargo helped to keep waterways traffic going but the freight charge had to be competitive, as these firms also had easy rail access. When Smart tried to charge Thomas Adams & Sons over the going rate, they returned his account saying: '*We cannot pay more than rail rate of 2s 11d*'.

If a boat arrived at Gloucester without a cargo and without having arranged a special one in advance, the crew took their turn at any one of the timber yards that had material to send up country. This was a very valuable fall-back option but at busy times it could involve a significant wait to load and it might mean having to go to an unpopular destination. When John Webb arrived at Gloucester expecting to load at Price, Walker's yard as usual, he found that there were ten boats already waiting there, so he wrote to James Smart asking

A Stroudwater boat at Gloucester in 1867, with Foster Brothers oil & cake mill on the right.

if he knew of anything else that needed doing, as he was concerned about not getting away before the Easter holidays, when some canals were stopped for maintenance. Several surviving letters written from Gloucester asked for money to be sent urgently, probably following a delay in loading. William Tenty wrote on a Tuesday asking for £6 10s to be sent to Gloucester Lock, in time for him to catch the first tug on Thursday morning, and H. Stephens wrote on a Thursday asking for five pounds to be sent to Diglis Lock, Worcester by Saturday morning.

Sailing ships in the Main Basin at Gloucester, viewed from the North Quay in 1883, a painting by Harley Crossley.

Occasionally, Smart was asked to load other cargoes at Gloucester. Two surviving letters from ship brokers Nurse Bros & Field asked for the cost of carrying slate and cement from Gloucester to Birmingham, and the same for wheat. Also, forwarding agents Reece & Barrett asked for the cost of sending glass sand from Sharpness to Birmingham, Brierley Hill and Spon Lane, adding that the sand must be kept dry. It may be this commodity that was being referred to in a letter from boatman Edward Eldridge, who reported from Gloucester that he had begun loading and that this would continue the next day. He wrote: '*You told me it would not want covering up, but you must send us some cloths tomorrow or Alfred will have to hire some. We borrowed some for tonight only. We had to get some slabs from Mr Wibby's for bottoms, also three or four bundles of straw. It is very particular stuff*'.

While waiting to be loaded, it seems that two boatmen may have had a disagreement. In one letter to James Smart, H. Gardner reported that he expected the boat to be loaded in two days' time but Gleed had gone missing and he (Gardner) did not have the key to the cabin. If Gleed would not come, Gardner asked Smart to send someone else and he also asked to be sent five pounds urgently. On one visit to Gloucester, J. Webb was asked by the bridgeman to load from a vessel in the dock rather than at a timber yard. So he wrote to Smart saying he would check with Price, Walker's in the morning and if not wanted there, he would do as the bridgeman asked. He added that he knew he would then have to wait for two boats and two barges to discharge before it was his turn and that he might not be home before Christmas.

After loading for Birmingham on 19th December 1893, Henry Stephens also expressed concern about not being able to discharge before Christmas, so he asked Smart to send

Boats in Gloucester Lock about to join the River Severn on their way 'up country'.
WA MH5

Boats at Gloucester's riverside quay, waiting to be towed up river by a steam tug.
GA SR25/31607.20GS

certain items for him to collect at the Bar Lock in Birmingham. While loading during another visit, Stephens asked Smart to send £10 or give it to his wife, who was due to come over by train. Having collected a cargo that had been left for him on the dockside, John Webb wrote to Smart expressing concern about the high wharfage charge he had been required to pay:

'If you comes to Gloucester, will you see some of the head ones about charging so much wharfage, 5s per boat, which brings the tonnage dearer than bringing it from Stroud'.

Under normal conditions, a boat loaded to go up country would be taken through Gloucester Lock and moored on the riverside quay, ready to be towed up the river in the morning. It was then usual for the boatmen to spend the evening visiting the local pubs. However, one time that James Smart's brother Jesse moored there near to his friend William Sisum, the night ended badly. After much drinking, both men returned to their boats, and when Smart tried to walk across the plank to his boat, he tumbled into the water. With much effort, he managed to scramble out and get on board. Next morning, however, Sisum was missing; his body was found in the Severn the following afternoon and at the inquest, the jury returned a verdict of 'found drowned'.

In January 1893, Henry Stephens was badly held up at Gloucester when the dock was frozen over for more than three weeks. William Staddon's boat was also held up but he had gone home. On 8th January, Stephens wrote to James Smart saying that no boats had been loaded yet and asked for one pound to be sent to Gloucester Lock. Ten days later, he reported: '*There is no prospect of us going away yet, as they have run the tug and knocked a hole in her and she can't break it, and they said they won't run any more unless they are paid for it. There is over 50 boats here, and about 10 trows to go when they start. They have got four tugs down here so they will soon shift some of them when they do start. We are all hard up. Will you please send me one pound. If you see Staddon, please tell him there is no hurry for him to come to the boat*'. In fact, the thaw set in the next day and everything slowly returned to normal.

For the passage up the River Severn, James Smart's boats were towed by one of the regular steam tugs and they would usually join up with other owners' barges and boats in the tow, often forming two lines. Each helmsman had to steer carefully, as the tug usually kept in the shallow water close to the bank to avoid the main flow of the river. Upper Lode Lock near Tewkesbury was big enough to take all the vessels in a tow, whilst at Diglis near Worcester, there were two locks side by side.

Once through Diglis Locks, most boats left the river to join the Worcester & Birmingham

Diglis Locks on the River Severn at Worcester in the 1890s, with a steam paddle tug exiting that had towed boats up the river.
WRO Acc. No. 27,231

A steam tug with six boats in tow (on two lines of three), approaching Bevere Lock on the Severn above Worcester circa 1910. The boat nearest the tug is laden with hay. NP

Canal but those with cargoes for the Black Country could continue up the river to Stourport and there join the Staffordshire & Worcestershire Canal. The usual procedure was for one member of the crew to be dropped off at Worcester to collect a horse and walk with it to Stourport as the boat was towed up river by a tug. On one occasion, however, John Webb found himself in a difficult position, as the man and horse never turned up. He sent a postcard to James Smart explaining what had happened and saying that he would go back down the road, hoping at least to find the horse. As he did not expect to find the man, he asked Smart to be ready to send a replacement following receipt of a confirmatory telegram.

The entrance lock from the River Severn on to the Worcester & Birmingham Canal, with a steam tug untying a boat brought up from Gloucester. NP

As it turned out, Webb soon sent another postcard saying the man had come. No explanation was given but it seems likely that the man had stopped too long at a pub and had spent the night sleeping it off.

For boats leaving the river at Worcester on their way up to Birmingham, there was another opportunity to report progress or to request instructions. In a typical postcard, Jesse Smart wrote asking his brother to send orders to the

Bar Lock, Birmingham, saying where he and William Staddon should go to load coal. George Crook wrote: '*We are loaded for Birmingham and shall get there tomorrow night. Please to send to the Canal Office, Birmingham, where we are to load when empty*'.

When going up the Worcester & Birmingham Canal, it was usual for James Smart's boatmen to hire two donkeys or sometimes a horse. The route included passing through four tunnels and working up the Tardebigge flight of thirty locks in two miles. On one trip, it seems that boatman Alfred Whiting fell ill while approaching Worcester Wharf, Birmingham, as he was taken to nearby Queens Hospital. He had been poorly on a previous trip ten months earlier when he had spent a whole day tied up but this time it was serious and he died of pneumonia on 22nd March 1894. Whiting had been one of James Smart's original boat captains back in the 1870s and he made a donation to the hospital to cover the cost of the funeral. For some

Two donkeys towing a boat on the Worcester & Birmingham Canal. WA R2156

Tardebigge Wharf, at the top of the climb through thirty-six locks from Stoke Prior. This circa 1910 view shows the steam tug provided to haul boats through the 580 yard long Tardebigge Tunnel. NP

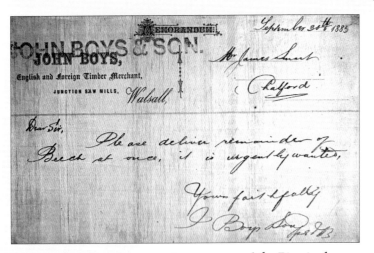

Letter from timber merchants John Boys & Son to James Smart. GA D4848 1885

Three horse boats moored at the top of the Farmers Bridge Locks in Birmingham. WA R0267B

reason, Whiting's boat remained where he had left it for at least a month and Smart had to arrange for it to be pumped out from time to time.

The timber carried up country was delivered to merchants who had waterside premises and so could benefit from transport direct by water, rather than have the timber brought up by rail to the nearest goods yard and then delivered by road. Surviving letters show James Smart had dealings with John Boys & Son of Walsall, George Rogers of Worcester Wharf, Birmingham, Rudder & Sons, Chester Street, Birmingham, and John Wilesmith of Worcester. No doubt there were many other customers around the Birmingham area and one letter refers to carrying timber to Coventry.

When a boat arrived at its destination, it was quite common for the captain to let Smart know when he expected his boat to be empty and to ask for instructions where he should go next. Some of these letters also referred to delays in discharging. One letter from Thomas Gardiner reported that he was emptying at Beddow's timber yard in Wolverhampton after a very long wait and he thought it was the worst place anywhere to discharge. He confirmed he would go to Cannock Chase to load coal for Wood & Rowe of Stroud, as Smart had told him. George Crook wrote: 'We had a week at Birmingham with the deals'. Walter Pearce reported that there had been a delay in unloading at Wolverhampton, as he had 'a midling place to put the heading and the wharf blocked up'. Henry Stephens reported from Birmingham that he should be unloaded in three days time but he was not sure as there were four boats in front. He asked Smart to let him know where to go next, as he was keen to move on after an enforced rest. John Webb reported that he had brought timber from Barkworth & Spaldin at Gloucester to the Corrugated Iron Company at Wolverhampton but there was a problem with discharging: 'We are here on strike as they wants us to carry the deals and stack them without pay, and I don't know how it will terminate.'

Some of the letters about discharging also gave information about other boatmen. One letter from John Webb reported that his boat was being unloaded at John Boys & Son's yard at Walsall but there had been difficulties in the way the round timber was being measured during discharge. He thought it should have been measured when being loaded and that it would have been better to have loaded deals, as Boys & Son did not seem to want the timber. He added that he and Crook would now go to Hednesford to load coal, unless Smart said otherwise, and he asked for them each to be sent nine or ten pounds. Walter Pearce reported from Birmingham that there were five boats at the yard before him and it would be two or three days before his boat would be empty. He added that James Davis was emptying at Camp Hill nearby and he asked that orders for both of them should be sent to the Bar Lock. When Smart wanted to know where Alfred Whiting was, Henry Stephens replied that Walter Pearce had told him on Thursday that Whiting had left Birmingham on Saturday heading for Cannock.

Horse boat part way down Farmers Bridge Locks in Birmingham. WA R0275

Some letters referred to not receiving an expected freight payment in cash for transporting the cargo. This could occur because the cargo was not considered up to specification or because the freight charge was included in the cost of the wood and needed to be collected from the Gloucester merchant. John Webb reported from Wolverhampton that the freight charge would have to be drawn at Gloucester and he offered to send the delivery note so Smart could collect the cash; otherwise he would call in for it on the way home. When Henry Stephens could not collect a freight charge in Birmingham, he also offered to send the delivery note but he recognised it might not be convenient for Smart to collect the cash, as his normal day for visiting Gloucester was a Saturday and the timber yard office would not then be open. When Alfred Whiting could not collect a freight charge, he wrote: *'Please send me £7 per return as I cannot get the freight until I get back to Gloucester. The horse has nothing to eat'*.

While on their way to or from the Midlands, boatmen occasionally helped James Smart's business by providing intelligence. Having talked with a potential customer who needed some ash poles moving, Smart's brother Jesse wrote from Birmingham that he believed they would get the job if they could match the railway rate of 10s per ton, as using boats would save the customer some haulage costs. When Henry Stephens reported that four

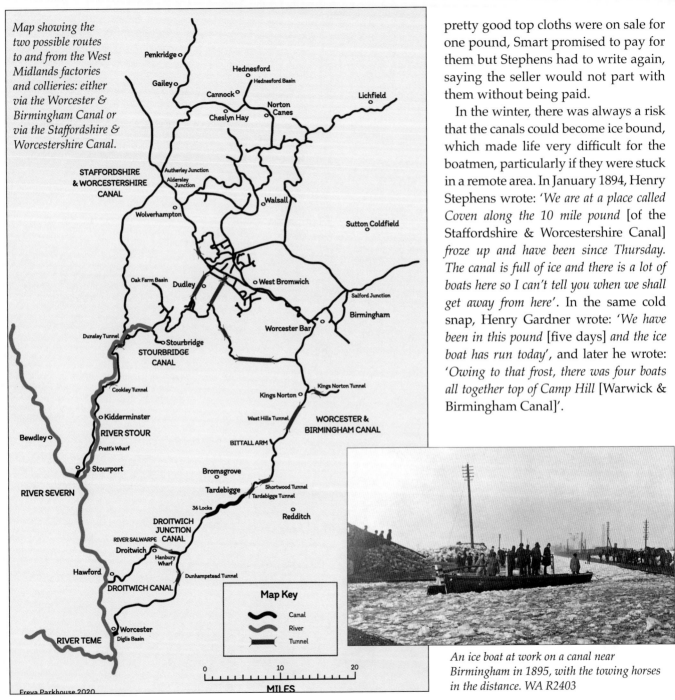

Map showing the two possible routes to and from the West Midlands factories and collieries: either via the Worcester & Birmingham Canal or via the Staffordshire & Worcestershire Canal.

pretty good top cloths were on sale for one pound, Smart promised to pay for them but Stephens had to write again, saying the seller would not part with them without being paid.

In the winter, there was always a risk that the canals could become ice bound, which made life very difficult for the boatmen, particularly if they were stuck in a remote area. In January 1894, Henry Stephens wrote: *'We are at a place called Coven along the 10 mile pound* [of the Staffordshire & Worcestershire Canal] *froze up and have been since Thursday. The canal is full of ice and there is a lot of boats here so I can't tell you when we shall get away from here'*. In the same cold snap, Henry Gardner wrote: *'We have been in this pound* [five days] *and the ice boat has run today'*, and later he wrote: *'Owing to that frost, there was four boats all together top of Camp Hill* [Warwick & Birmingham Canal]*'*.

An ice boat at work on a canal near Birmingham in 1895, with the towing horses in the distance. WA R2403

~ 22 ~

Chapter 3

Return from the Midlands

O nce James Smart's boats had delivered their outward cargo in the Midlands, most went on to load coal at one of the collieries on Cannock Chase. These included East Cannock, Cannock Chase and Cannock & Wimblebury collieries around Hednesford Basin. Conduit Colliery No. 3 (known as 'Jerome') was at Norton Canes on the Cannock Extension Canal and the Cannock Old Coppice Colliery (known as 'Hawkins') was at Cheslyn Hay, on the Hatherton Branch of the Staffordshire & Worcestershire Canal. In 1882, prices quoted by collieries varied from 9s per ton for large coal to 3s 6d per ton for slack; by 1896, the equivalent range was from 12s 6d to 5s per ton. It was well known that collieries commonly loaded more coal into a boat than they charged for, which, it seems, was formally acknowledged in 1893 when the Conduit Colliery quoted prices per ton of 2,400lbs rather than for the standard ton of 2,240lbs.

The choice of where to go and what type of coal to collect was sometimes left to the last moment, as several surviving letters are from boatmen asking for instructions about such matters to be sent to them while en route. While waiting to discharge timber in January 1894, Henry Stephens wrote: *'Will you please send orders to me care Messrs Rudder & Sons,*

Conduit Colliery No. 3 at Norton Canes circa 1910. The canal basin, which boatmen referred to as 'Jerome', was just out of the picture to the left. NP

Coal boats at the 'Jerome' basin around 1900, which served Conduit Colliery No. 3. The photograph graphically illustrates just how labour intensive this work was, with four or five men loading every boat.
WA BW192/3/2/2/2/69

A Conduit Colliery receipted invoice for coal and slack dated 1882.
GA D4367/2/2 C01

No.
CONDUIT COLLIERY, BROWNHILLS,
9th Nove 1882

Mr Jos Smart—

Bought of The Conduit Colliery Compy.

	T.	C.	Rate.	£	s.	d.
Shallow Coal, Large						
Slack						
Deep Coal, Colliery	23	-	10/	11	10	-
Slack	11	-	3/6	1	18	6
Bass Coal, Large				13	8	6
Slack						

Received by

Chester Street, Birmingham.' George Crook wrote: '***Charity*** *will be empty tomorrow. We shall go to Cannock Chase if there is no orders to the contrary.'* One letter from Eastington coal merchant Zaccheus Whiting asked if a boat could be diverted to load for him: '*If you are likely to load Old Side Hednesford or Wimblebury, I should be glad with another boat load. If W Pearce is not ordered, could you kindly write him to load for me Hednesford if can. If can't, to try to get a good load Gerome* [Jerome]'. When there were labour difficulties in the pits, James Davis wrote that he would check the morning paper and if there was no news of the collieries going in, he would return home.

Some of the requests for orders or for money emphasised the need for clear information, suggesting that there had been difficulties in the past. Walter Pearce wrote from Wolverhampton: *'Please send orders at once to Hednesford what we are to load with. Please send us £12 at the same time. If we are to load slack, please say what sort of slack'*. Jesse Smart wrote from Birmingham: *'Please send me a cheque for £10 for Monday morning certain. Please address Jesse Smart, Norton Canes post office, Nr Cannock, Staffordshire, and direct the letter right this time to prevent me being delayed'*. John Webb wrote from Birmingham: *'Will you please send by return of post to Bar Lock where we are to go to load. If we got to load bricks, what yard it is and what sort'*.

At a colliery where James Smart did not have an account, the coal had to be paid for at the time of collection and several surviving letters include a reminder asking him to send money in good time, to avoid a delay in loading. William Staddon wrote: *'If we got to bring much Deeps you must send the money accordingly'*. Alfred Whiting wrote: *'Please send the orders by return of post. Also please send the money for the coal to the colliery'*. James Davis wrote: *'It would be much better if you would send the money as we could pay for the coal. Please to send as I can have it on Tuesday morning'* and on another occasion, *'If there is any money required for the coal at Geroam [Jerome], please send by return of post to Geroam'*.

While at a colliery, it was common for a boatman to report progress to James Smart, often with a request for money to be sent. John Webb wrote from Hednesford: *'We have been loading slack and black ones at the Old Side and we got a good load of stuff on. I can't tell whether we shall be home this week or no, but if not this week, we shall be on Monday. Will you kindly let my wife have a pound to settle up my club, if she wants it, as I shall want all that I have got to bring the boat home'*. Alfred Whiting wrote from Hednesford: *'We arrived here this morning and shall be loaded either Friday night or first thing Saturday morning. Please send five pounds by return of post as I expect we shall be waiting for it'*. On another trip, Whiting wrote from Conduit Colliery: *'I shall want you to send me five pounds to the Bar Lock, Gas St, Birmingham. Please to send a post office order for I shall not be able to cash a cheque. Send it by return of post for we shall be at Birmingham on Wednesday morning'*. The amount of coal loaded into a boat could be limited by the depth of water in the canals and on one trip Walter Pearce thought it worth warning Smart: *'The water is very low in the canal but we shall bring as good a load as we possibly can'*.

The logo of the Cannock & Rugeley Colliery Co. Ltd, from a letterhead dated 1893. MiP 2008.74/47

The Cannock & Rugeley Colliery Co's East Cannock colliery, which fed coal via a tramway down to Hednesford basin for canal boats to load. JR

A pre-First World War view of the salt works at Stoke Prior, with the Worcester & Birmingham Canal running through the centre, behind the clock tower. NP

Colliery loading men must have become familiar with the regular boatmen, so when James Davis was running short of money at Cannock & Rugeley Colliery, rather than contact Smart himself, he got the loading supervisor to write asking for him to be sent six pounds. At Cannock Old Coppice Colliery, George Crook obtained an advance on his wages, promising James Smart would settle the debt but six weeks later the colliery had to write to Smart: '*I think you have overlooked the £2 10s we advanced to Crook in August last. Will you kindly remit same and we shall be glad to see your boats here oftener*'.

From time to time, James Smart wanted a boat to call in at Stoke Prior on the way home usually to pick up one ton of salt. As this meant space had to be left when loading coal, several surviving letters include a request for instructions as to whether any salt was needed or not. Walter Pearce wrote from Conduit Colliery: '*We are at Jerome. Load about Thursday. Send back if you want any salt*'. On another trip, Pearce wrote: '*I shall bring a ton of salt if we don't get much more rain*'. From Conduit Colliery, Henry Stephens wrote: '*We shall be able to bring 3 or 4 tons of salt if you want it because the canal* [here] *is very low so we shall not be able to load so very deep. Let me know if that will be too much salt*'.

Several surviving letters refer to complaints made by James Smart to the Cannock & Rugeley Colliery Company, which illustrate the difficulties of managing activities at a distance. When Smart complained that a cargo was one ton short, the loading supervisor accepted Smart's word and agreed to make an allowance on the next cargo, as the existing

record had already gone through to the
office. However, when Smart complained
that he had been charged more for a
load than the company had quoted, the
loading supervisor pointed out that the
quotation had been for coal in trucks,
not loaded into boats. Also, when Smart
complained about the quality of a load of
slack, the loading supervisor explained:
*'Capt Pearce said he wanted Rough Slack but
to put the fine slack in with it to make it come
cheaper. This we did, and I charged the fine in
it. If I had known you wanted Engine Slack, I
could have had it loaded in that way'.* When

*Loading bricks at
Amblecote on the
Stourbridge Canal.
WA R0272.*

Smart asked for a price reduction, the supervisor replied: *'I regret the slack was not suitable but
at the same time it was loaded according to your order. I am sorry I cannot reduce the price as others
are paying the same and we have a great demand for it'.*

Although most trips to the Midlands involved collecting coal, James Smart's boats were
also called upon to carry bricks to the Stroud Valley. Surviving correspondence shows Smart
had dealings with brick makers Wood & Ivery of West Bromwich, S.J. Sadler of Oldbury and
Hickman & Co. of Stourbridge, as well as receiving quotations from other companies. From

THE LEAR COOKLEY

*A pair of donkeys feed
from their nose cans as
they haul a narrowboat
south towards Stourport
along the Staffordshire
& Worcestershire Canal
at Cookley, around 1910.
The bridge, built in 1904,
carried waterpipes from
the Elan Valley reservoir
to Birmingham. NP*

ON THE SEVERN AT STOURPORT

Boats moored in the River Severn at Stourport around 1906, by the lock entrance to the basin, which then led on to the Staffordshire & Worcestershire Canal.
NP

one letter, however, it appears that more boats were sent to Wood & Ivery's brickworks than they could cope with, as they were also supplying customers by rail. John Webb wrote to Smart: '*Thanks to your brother, there is nothing for us to load. I can't think what made him load two boats, and Walter will be here tomorrow and it will take him all this week to get away as they are going to send* [some] *by rail*'. Webb evidently remembered this incident as, when on his way for a return visit, he wrote: '*I wish we could have went to Hawkins* [colliery], *but I suppose* [Stroudwater manager] *Snape wants the bricks. I hope they will be ready after going back*'. An infrequent but regular return cargo was fire bricks and retorts for Stroud Gas Works. These provided a good profit, in spite of a high toll charge on the Stroudwater Canal, because there was no rail access to the gas works until 1924.

Other less common homeward cargoes are recorded in the Stroudwater Canal tonnage books. In the late 1880s, when highways authorities were looking for harder stone than available from the Bristol gorge or Chepstow, James Smart's boats collected granite road stone from Rowley Regis, until it was found more economical to bring stone from Cornwall. In 1887, Smart's boats collected iron pipes from the Midlands, for new water mains along the

Stroud Valley. In June 1889, three boats brought 65 tons of birch planks from Liverpool to Chalford, whilst later that year three boats also brought coal from Polesworth to Chalford. In the 1880s, foundry sand from near Stourport was delivered to Brimscombe Foundry and in the 1890s to Thrupp Foundry. For two years from 1896, Smart's boats carried soda ash from Northwich in Cheshire to Dudbridge, from where it was taken overland to a borax factory at Inchbrook, near Nailsworth. Going further afield, William Staddon's son remembered visiting Leicestershire, Northampton and Nottingham by

A tug tows a pair of narrowboats down river beneath Holt Fleet bridge. The vessels have just exited Holt Fleet Lock, which is hidden by the bush in the right foreground. DM

canal. In addition, one surviving letter shows that Smart was planning to collect some machinery from Hebden Bridge in Yorkshire.

Once loaded with coal, most boats returned home through Birmingham but some surviving letters refer to returning via Stourport, a longer distance but with fewer locks. From Hednesford, Walter Pearce wrote: '*If you want to write to us, you can write to Stourport*'. Henry Stephens wrote: '*We are coming back Stour Road. Will you please send me £2 to Canal Office, Stourport*'. Edward Eldridge reported that he was running late, because Alfred Whiting had been taken bad, causing them to stay tied up for a day, after which the Stour Canal was very low. Walter Pearce had evidently intended to return via Stourport but he sent a postcard saying that the Churchbridge Locks were stopped and so he came the Birmingham way.

One factor in the choice of route was whether the loading colliery was to the west of the huge Churchbridge flight of locks, as was the case at Cannock Old Coppice Colliery (known as 'Hawkins'). This favoured the route to Stourport and a long run down the Severn but if the upper river was in flood, there was a need for a long rope, known as a Severn line, for dragging a heavy piece of iron to slow the boat down when drifting through bridges. J. Webb evidently did not want to pay for a Severn line, as he wrote: '*We should come back through Birmingham as there will be a big flood and we got no rope*'. George Crook wrote: '*I shall pay for the Severn line, and I shall want you to send me two pounds to Stourport post office*'. When Walter Pearce was concerned about using the upper river in flood, he chose to load coal at a colliery which suited a return via Birmingham and Worcester. Knowing that the different coal might not suit the intended customer, he wrote to Smart: '*We are at Jerome. I should went to Hawkins, but I was afraid of being flooded as we have not got any rope any good. Charles Smith said Whiting [at Eastington] would have this load of coal if you did not want it. Please let me know*'.

Boats at the north portal of Wast Hills Tunnel on the Worcester & Birmingham Canal, waiting for the tug to take them through.

For those returning through Birmingham, surviving letters show that there could be delays if water levels were low, causing boats to drag along the bottom. After a particularly slow journey, Walter Pearce wrote: *'We thought of having Saturday tug, but we was from Wednesday one o'clock till ten on Thursday night getting to Birmingham. We were on the bottom all the way. I don't think we ever had a worser job to get along. Now we shan't have till Monday's tug'*. On another trip, on 20th January 1894, Pearce wrote: *'We've been two days and a night getting to Birmingham as the canal is half dry as they pumps it out as fast as it rains in'*. When Jesse Smart was similarly delayed, he wrote: *'The water is so low on some parts of the Birmingham Canal. We should have had Saturday morning's tug down Severn. As it is, we shall try and drift down on Sunday* [when no tug running], *and all being well we shall be down on Monday night. Please let my wife know'*.

Another source of delay prompted Walter Pearce to write: *'We had an awkward job to get along the top level. We had to tie up all day yesterday on account of the fog. Two of Pearce's boats met with accidents by a smashed helm and a broken gunwhale. We shall have Monday's tug if the water is not too big* [in the Severn]. *I think we have two very good loads of coal'*. James Davis was having better luck when he wrote: *'We are at Birmingham and shall have the tug on Saturday if all's well. Please send me £2 by return of post to Mr Wilmott, lock keeper, Diglis'*. After another slow trip, William Tenty asked: *'Please send me £1 to the Canal Office, Diglis,*

Worcester, by return of post as I have not got one shilling left'.

Surviving letters from Worcester show it was common for boatmen to let James Smart know which tug they intended to go with down the river to Gloucester. However, one letter from Henry Stephens was more concerned with obtaining money that was not waiting for him as he had requested. He wrote: *'You have not sent me any money so I have not got any. Will you please send me three pounds to Mr George Harris, Severn [Commission] office, [Gloucester]. If you send it before 10 o'clock, I shall get it in the afternoon'.* More usual letters included,

Half Way, Bromsgrove.

from James Davis: *'We shall leave here first tug on Monday morning'*, and from George Crook: *'**Charity** will come down Severn in the morning'*. Walter Pearce wrote: *'We arrived at Worcester on Sunday night. We shall have Monday morning tug. If I do not hear from you, we come up home'*.

Half Way House was a farm with a licence beside the Worcester & Birmingham Canal near Bromsgrove, named because it was the halfway point along the thirty-six locks down from Tardebigge to Stoke Prior. NP

Gloucester from the Severn.

A steam tug and its tow rounding a sharp bend on the approach to Gloucester circa 1905. NP

A boat loaded with coal heads south from Gloucester circa 1885, probably on its way to the Stroud Valley. NP

Other letters from Worcester reported delays due to adverse weather. J. Webb wrote: '*We came here yesterday morning, but the water is all over the country and blowing hard, so I don't know when we shall get down*'. George Crook wrote: '*We are in Worcester* [lock] *cutting and ought to have come down Severn on Monday, but some of them said there would be another tug on Tuesday morning which would be better than starting from here at half past twelve. But the frost came on so severe that the tugs could not come. There was a lot of people skating on the Severn above Worcester Bridge on Wednesday. The ice was five inches thick here on some of the clay holes on Wednesday. I have sent for the money you sent to Gloucester and received it. The boat, donkeys and coal is all right at present*'.

As James Smart's boats delivered to wharfs all along the Stroudwater and Thames & Severn canals, some letters from Worcester asked for instructions if any cargo needed to be discharged on the way back to Chalford. Henry Stephens wrote: '*If you want us to put any coal out anywhere below Chalford, will you please send us a postcard to the Junction or Gloucester*'.

THE CANAL AT EASTINGTON E357

A boat approaching Pike Lock on the Stroudwater Canal at Eastington, virca 1908. NP

Walter Pearce wrote: '*Please send a postcard to Gloster where we have got to unload if you know*'. John Webb wrote: '*We got three knees of lumps and the rest coal. If you want any put out anywhere below* [Chalford], *please have the barrows and scales ready*'.

When discharging, it was common to shovel the coal into a hand barrow, which two men could lift and carry to where it was to be stacked. However, when a crew returned home late in the day, they naturally tied the boat up and went home for the night, expecting to discharge the following morning. One night, a policeman walking along the towpath saw something moving on one of James Smart's boats; he later stopped two youths who were carrying bags full of coal. At Stroud police court, they pleaded guilty and elected to be tried summarily. They were bound over in the sum of £5 for six months to come up for judgement when called upon.

To ensure that living conditions on canal boats were not unhealthy, each boat had to be inspected and registered with a local health authority, who placed a limit on how many people could occupy the cabin. Boats were liable to spot checks, which could be

Discharging coal at Brimscombe using a hand barrow.

carried out at any point on their voyage. In one surviving letter to James Smart, the City of Birmingham Health Department threatened prosecution because a case of overcrowding on the boat **Industry** had not been remedied. Smart evidently knew that health authorities were reluctant to prosecute, so it was not until the Stroud Local Board also issued a notice of overcrowding four months later that the matter was resolved. Around the same time, Smart was threatened with prosecution for not producing a registration certificate for the boat **Serapis**. When he did produce the certificate, it emerged that the boat needed to be re-registered, and subsequently he was given a time and a place for it to be inspected.

Chapter 4

Forest & Vale

As well as sending boats to the Midlands for coal, another aspect of James Smart's business was collecting cargoes from places nearer to home, including the Forest of Dean coal outlets at Bullo and Lydney docks, and the larger docks at Gloucester and Sharpness. Bullo Pill was a major source of coal delivered to places along the Stroud Valley and further east, as a result of which Smart was in competition with several other carriers for the business. For this traffic, Smart mainly used his barges but his boats also made the tricky trip across the Severn when required.

Many surviving letters concern James Smart buying Forest of Dean coal direct from a colliery, arranging for its delivery to Bullo or Lydney docks and then paying for it. Smart dealt with several collieries, including Buckholt, Littledean Woodside, Lydney & Crump Meadow, Parkend Deep Navigation and Speech House. Depending on the colliery, grades were given names such as 'Best Blocks', 'Lumps', 'Rubbles', 'Nuts', 'Steam Coal', 'Lime Coal', 'Thro & Thro', 'Engine Culm' and 'Slack'. In March 1893, pit head prices quoted by the Parkend Deep Navigation Colliery were 11s 3d to 12s 3d per ton for house coal and 6s 3d per ton for steam coal, plus 6d per ton for use of colliery trucks, with the assurance that: *'We have now changed our method of screening Hand-picked Block and Rubbles and that these two descriptions are much improved in size and freedom from small'*.

Other surviving letters concern James Smart buying Forest coal through various coal agents. These included Gollop & Co. of Lydney and James Smith of Stroud, who was a director of the Trafalgar Colliery Co. but Smart had most contact with Bernard Edwards of Gloucester. Letters from Edwards reported on matters such as there being plenty of coal at the dock to be collected, that a specific order was on its way to the dock, that the coal shipper had been asked to load Smart's barge promptly and how much coal had been loaded in a particular barge. When Smart complained that one

Barge delivering coal to Ryeford coal pen. Note the wooden boards in the hold, used to separate different grades of coal, and the iron stanchions which supported a pole carrying a protective side cloth when on the move. MM

load was of poor quality, Edwards assured him that: '*nothing but Lumps were loaded and it was carefully weighed on a scales*', adding '*I think when you get it home, you will be satisfied with it*'. Occasionally, Edwards recommended a special deal to help reduce the stock of coal held at Bullo. One letter offered: '*a cargo of really good rough lime coal, Trafalgar, Crump Meadow, New Bowson mixed. I have 100 tons at Bullo that I will clear at once at 5s 3d free on board. I make you the first offer. It is very good*'.

As well as buying coal to sell on to his customers, James Smart also did a good business carrying coal for other local firms, who had ordered direct from a colliery or for an agent selling direct to a customer. Agent Bernard Edwards inquired what charge Smart would make for carrying around eighteen cargoes per year from Bullo to Ashby's Yard, Gloucester, including hauling 150 yards from the canal side. Edwards also arranged for Smart to send a trial load of Bullo coal to Gloucester Gas Works, liaising with the haulier who would

The entrance to the Stroudwater Canal at Framilode was the way to and from Bullo Pill, which was about five miles down the River Severn from this point.

help discharge it. Agent James Smith used Smart as a carrier, as well as sometimes selling him coal for his own customers. One time, when Smart sent an account for carrying with a request for a cheque, Smith replied with a larger account for the coal Smart had purchased recently and asked him to settle the difference. Another confusion led the Buckholt Colliery Co. to ask Smart whether a load of coal shipped in **Perseverance** should be charged to Smart or to the recipients.

James Smart's coal business was disturbed during 1893, when there was a period of unrest in the coalfields all over the country. In response to falling house coal prices, coal owners tried to reduce wages but the colliers resisted and many collieries shut down temporarily. However, Smart received a letter from the Speech House Company saying they intended to stay open as long as they could and encouraged their customers to take '*a reasonable and early supply of coal*'. In spite of this, there was a marked shortage of supply for three months until the local dispute was settled, whilst difficulties continued for a further three months before there was a national return to work.

Most of the Forest coal carried by James Smart's vessels was loaded at Bullo Pill Dock, about five miles down the River Severn from the entrance to the Stroudwater Canal at Framilode. Both places were only accessible around the time of the spring tides and the voyage between them was only possible during a seven day period every fortnight. However, a pair of riverside tips were also provided at Box Meadow Wharf, a couple of hundred yards to the south of the entrance to Bullo Dock, which negated vessels having to wait for the tides to be right for entering or leaving the dock itself. This short but tricky passage was frequently made by Smart's barge *Perseverance*, which could raise its sails when in the open water. The passage was also made by some of his narrowboats, which mainly drifted with the tide. To provide some steerage way relative to the tidal flow, a boat was led by a rowing boat ahead or was held back by dragging a heavy piece of metal on the end of a long rope.

At Bullo, a captain was told to put his vessel under the tip where the coal ordered for him was tipped on board; before leaving he was given a lock ticket by the shipping agent saying how much had been loaded. Sometimes, mistakes were made and James Smart later received a letter with a corrected ticket. Smart also received letters from his captains reporting reasons for delay, such as a very thick fog or the river being full of ice, whilst one captain asked for an advance on his wages to be sent to his home in Arlingham, to which he had walked via the Newnham ferry.

One desperate letter from John Webb reported that he was stuck at Bullo two days before Christmas and the tide window had passed. The coal he had come for had been discharged from wagons at the Bullo Wagon Works. When the mistake was realised, the

Edward Paget-Tomlinson's 1997 painting of a trow loading coal at Bullo Dock in the early years of the 20th century. NP

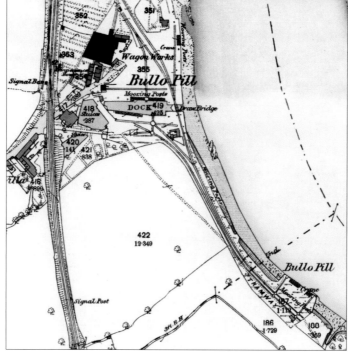

Bullo Pill dock and Box Meadow Wharf, as shown on the 1st Edition 1880 25 inch OS.

*The trow **Mystery** loading coal at Box Meadow Wharf, Bullo, in the 1890s. (The image has previously been associated with Chepstow but the jetty does not match anything known to exist there and the backgound is wrong for the River Wye.)*
NMM B2951

A typical Stroud barge with single mast and open hold approaching the Stroudwater entrance at Framilode.
GA SRPRINTS/126A.8GS

coal had been put back in the wagons with a view to loading it into Webb's boat but he thought it was nothing but a load of slack. He had asked for some patent fuel instead but the shipper said nothing could be loaded without orders and Smart had not replied to an earlier telegram. With the tides falling away and a strong wind blowing down the river, Webb did not want to load what he feared could not be delivered. He said he would return home for Christmas, expecting that someone would pay for the boat being stuck at Bullo.

Although coal was the main cargo carried from Bullo, James Smart's boats and barges also collected some loads of crushed furnace slag for the County Council to use on the roads in place of stone. Unfortunately, surviving letters show that there were some administrative difficulties in setting up this traffic. Initially, James Smart asked the Cinderford Crushing Company to get 500 tons ready to be loaded at Bullo during the following week, with the company reporting three days later that 72 tons had been sent by rail to Bullo and the rest would be sent in the following days. By then, however, Smart had heard that the County Council wanted urgent delivery, which meant ordering stone to be sent by train to Brimscombe and he told the Crushing Company not to send any more slag to Bullo. This prompted the Company to ask what they should do about the special end tipping wagons that they had hired and the extra men they had put on to load them, and they particularly requested Smart to collect the 135 tons of slag then at Bullo or the demurrage on the wagons could exceed the value of their contents. Smart sent his barge *Perseverance* to collect some of the slag but then there was further delay whilst he was contacted to clarify who would pay the shipping cost. Once these early difficulties were overcome, the remainder of the original order was collected over the following months.

When returning from Bullo to Framilode, a barge could use its sails but a boat just drifted with the tide with a rowing boat ahead or a heavy weight trailing behind. In particularly windy conditions, an extra boatman could be hired to assist in the rowing boat but on one occasion, the captain only paid the extra man a fraction of the going rate and he had to write to Smart to claim the rest. Because the passage depended on the tides, boats sometimes arrived at Framilode during the night. William Staddon's son remembered one occasion, when they got there at midnight on a Saturday, his father said: '*It's no good staying here, we may as well toddle home*'. So they walked the sixteen miles to Chalford, then on Monday morning they walked back to Framilode by 7.00am.

*The barge **Irene** in Framilode Basin circa 1908. This route out on to the Severn fell out of use in the 1920s. NP*

The Upper Basin at Lydney, seen here circa 1910 with a selection of small wooden sailing ships loading or waiting to load Forest of Dean coal. NP

The Docks, Lydney. (No. 2)

As well as loading at Bullo, James Smart's barges also collected Forest coal from Lydney Docks, just across the river from Sharpness. *Perseverance* was a regular visitor, and *Flora* and *Industry* called occasionally. Usually the coal was destined for delivery in the Stroud Valley but Smart was asked to send one load of 'Brick' coal to Walham Brick Works, beside the river north of Gloucester. Usually the barges went empty to Lydney but occasionally they carried wooden boxes specially made for carrying the tin plate that was manufactured at Richard Thomas's works near the docks.

Shipments of coal from Lydney declined after the Sharpness Dock Company built a big coal tip for seagoing ships beside their new dock in 1885 and the original coal tip in the old dock was dedicated for use by smaller vessels. After this, it became increasingly common for James Smart's barges to load at Sharpness rather than make the short but tricky voyage to Lydney. Shipments of coal and furnace slag from Bullo continued for a few years but these had almost died out by 1900.

Very occasionally, James Smart was asked to collect a cargo from an open wharf on the west side of the river. In 1890, the barge *Perseverance* made numerous trips to Newnham to collect round timber and the narrowboat *Hugh Percy* also made several trips during the same period. When timber merchant John Merrett wanted larch and spruce tree trunks to be loaded at Woolaston, Smart asked his captain Henry Meadows to investigate while he was visiting nearby Lydney to deliver wooden boxes. Meadows walked down to where

the timber was lying, reporting back that they would have to wait for a big spring tide to be able to get a barge in close; *Perseverance* subsequently made two trips to collect the logs. On another trip, the same vessel visited Broadoak to deliver a shed that coal agent Bernard Edwards had bought in Gloucester and needed moving to his home in Elton. One of Smart's barges also visited Collow Wharf, south of Newnham, where there was evidently some difficulty as Smart ended up paying the owner's claim for damages.

Other occasional visits were made to collect timber from places up river from Gloucester. In 1880, *Perseverance* picked up a load from Tewkesbury and in 1888 from Apperley. In 1885, Thomas Gardiner reported great difficulty in collecting timber from Upton on Severn, as it was a long way from the riverside and he had to pay men to help load it. He wrote: *'We shall try and come down to Gloucester on Sunday and get home on Monday if we possibly can'* and he added: *'I want you to send me ten shillings to Gloucester Lock by return of post as I shall not have enough money to pay the Berkeley tonnage after I have paid the men for helping us to load'*. In 1880, Smart's boats visited the Hereford & Gloucester Canal to load timber

With little freeboard showing, the heavily loaded barge **Finis** *is seen moored to the bank at Broadoak, near Newnham around 1910. Two crewmen can be made out handbarrowing off a delivery probably of coal along a pair of what look to be perilously balanced planks – but they will have done this many times before. NP*

from Hereford and from Newent. In the early 1890s, several loads of timber were collected from Forthampton for saw millers E. Gregory & Sons of Berkeley. One letter from Gregory explained that he had paid the captains £14 13s in cash, which would reduce the amount payable to Smart, and he asked when a boat would be back at Forthampton as he needed to arrange horses to move the timber. In a later letter, following a misunderstanding, Gregory accepted that timber ordered to Berkeley Pill could be delivered to Shepherds Patch on the Sharpness Canal, where it could be dealt with by saw miller Francis Morgan of Cambridge.

Another source of cargoes for James Smart's boats and barges was Gloucester Docks, from where many consignments of imported corn and timber needed to be carried to the Stroud Valley and beyond. Smart kept the narrowboat *Thomas* running a shuttle service between Gloucester and Chalford, with occasional stops in between, and other boats could be laid

The Docks, Gloucester.

on when required. Surviving letters from timber merchants include one from Nicks & Co., who wanted a boat to take 15 tons to builder George Shaylor of Brimscombe, and another from Price, Walker & Co., who wanted to send 18 tons to builders Drew Bros of Chalford. However, the demand for these local deliveries was very variable and it was difficult to keep everyone happy. At one busy time, timber merchant Francis Vibert threatened that if Smart's boat did not arrive soon, he would put his boards an another boat. Then, on another day, boatman H. Gardiner found there was no timber to load at Gloucester, so rather than wait in hope, he wrote to Smart asking if

The travelling crane at Baltic Wharf, to the south of the main docks at Gloucester, around 1900. NP

there was any other cargo he could pick up, as he wanted to get home on Saturday.

One load of birch timber for Chalford took over a month to make the journey, as the boat became stuck in ice in Whitminster Lock just before Christmas 1890. Captain Jesse Smart and mate William Staddon junior stabled the horse and went home to Chalford but they had to visit the boat regularly to check that the ice was not cutting into the hull. Young Staddon later remembered that at Chalford the ice was very thick and there were sway boats and bonfires on the ice. Towards the end of January, the ice began to thaw but the crew's troubles were not at an end. As they were fetching the horse, it stumbled and fell into the canal, only a quarter of a mile from the boat. It was impossible to save it from drowning and the unfortunate beast had to be pulled from the water with the help of another horse and a noose. Lord Fitzhardinge had the carcass for the Berkeley Hounds and Jesse Smart had to send for another horse to pull their boat home.

The Stroudwater Canal and Lodgemore Mill pond at Downfield, Stroud frozen over in 1881. During such icy spells, the mill pond was a popular place for skating. MM

Some of James Smart's boats left Gloucester with multiple consignments of different materials for different places. For example, in 1888, the narrowboat *Serapis* carried 3 tons of boards to Eastington; 7 tons of timber, 1 ton of petroleum and 10 tons of corn to Chalford; and 2 tons of cake to Kempsford. A few years later, boatman William Tenty carried loads for six different people at Ebley and Brimscombe. Other notable cargoes included a 16-ton boiler to Chalford and also 90 tons of borate of lime carried by three boats to Dudbridge, for the borax factory at Inchbrook near Nailsworth. One unofficial consignment comprised three walking sticks sent by Gloucester lockkeeper Charles Edwards to a Chalford craftsman, each with a label saying what he wanted done.

Although most of the traffic from Gloucester was to nearby destinations, some of James Smart's boats carried imported timber over the Cotswolds for firms such as Price, Walker & Co., Nicks & Co. and Thomas Adams & Co. For many years, there were shipments of deals to Oxford and timber and grain to Swindon, and for limited periods deals were sent to Reading and boards were taken to Chippenham. One boat carrying deals to Reading also dropped off a plough at Chalford.

As well as cargoes arranged in advance by correspondence, James Smart obtained some business through arrangements made by his captains dealing with the merchants they visited. While waiting to load timber for Ebley at Nicks & Co's yard at Gloucester, boatman Walter Pearce wrote: '*They have got a full load for Mr Harper* [of Cainscross] *here, and I have*

.The Docks, Sharpness. .932.

Sharpness main dock from the High Level Swing Bridge circa 1900. NP

promised to come back and fetch it unless you have got anything else for us better. There will be another half load nearly at Price's for Gardiner and Shaylor [at Chalford], *and we shall leave about five tons here for Ebley. I promised Price's that you would have a boat there on Tuesday'.*

Another source of cargoes for Smart's boats was Sharpness Dock, whence many boats carried imported grain to Stroud, Chalford, Lechlade and intermediate places. Some consignments had to be collected overside from a steamer and surviving letters report timing difficulties. Boatman Henry Stephens wrote that two boats were at Sharpness but the steamer they were due to load from had not arrived. After one letter from corn merchants Thomas Robinson & Co. asked for a boat to be at Sharpness to meet a steamer that needed to discharge quickly, they wrote again four days later to say the steamer had gone to Bristol instead. Boatman William Gardiner reported that he had loaded 80 sacks of maize but he would have to wait a day while the beans that were part of the order were washed.

Some ships arriving at Sharpness brought more goods for the Stroud Valley than could be carried by one barge and Smart was under pressure to provide the right number of boats and barges to ensure the ship could discharge without delay. In 1889, several consignments of manganese ore for paint makers S.G. Bailey & Co. of Stafford Mill arrived in schooners from Plymouth and each required three or four vessel movements to collect the cargoes. Also that year, a steamer from Liverpool brought 227 tons of birch planks for walking stick manufacturer W. Dangerfield & Co. of Chalford, and it took two barges and four narrowboats to move it all in one day.

After the Sharpness Dock Company built a big coal tip for seagoing ships beside their new dock in 1885, the original tip in the old dock was dedicated for use by smaller vessels and it became increasingly common for James Smart's barges to load coal at Sharpness rather than Lydney. This trend was enhanced as shipments from Bullo declined during the 1890s. Few letters have survived about this growing traffic but one from coal agent Bernard Edwards reported that there was a difference of 4 tons between the Dock Company's weighing machine and the Great Western Railway one at Awre. Another letter asked Smart to quote for carrying 5,000 tons of coal from Sharpness to Gloucester Gas Works over a period of twelve months, whilst another offered to supply small steam coal at Sharpness at 7s 4d per ton.

A few trips for James Smart's boats and barges only involved places along the Gloucester & Sharpness Canal. A postcard from Gloucester timber merchant John Merrett asked Smart to collect a barge load of poles from Parkend Bridge while the weather remained fine. A card from Fawkes Bros, corn & cake merchants, asked Smart to collect some sacks of beans from Packthorne Farm (near Saul Junction) and deliver to Spillers & Bakers at Gloucester. Writing from Gloucester, captain Alfred Meadows reported that *Flora* would be leaving Gloucester in the afternoon carrying ashes to Sharpness. No doubt there were many other such local trips but the records have not survived.

From the late 1880s, a common trip for Smart's boats and barges involved loading a cargo at Saul Junction from a vessel that had come up the Gloucester & Sharpness Canal but was

The old coal tip at Sharpness on 22nd August 1964, where Stroudwater boats loaded Forest of Dean coal brought over via the Severn Railway Bridge. BP/KRM

too big to continue up the Stroudwater Canal. There was no wharf at the Junction, so the vessel moored in the basin and the goods were lowered into a boat alongside. In 1887, three boats carried road stone from the Junction to Cirencester and four carried oak timber to Ryeford Saw Mill.

The road stone traffic developed in the early 1890s when the local highways authorities were looking for harder stone than was readily available from Bristol or Chepstow. Normally, Smart was given advance notice of when the ship was due and again, he was expected to have boats ready so the ship could be discharged quickly. If he did not have enough boats available, the remainder of the cargo was discharged at Frampton Wharf, three-quarters of a mile down the Sharpness Canal, and Smart's boats collected from there when they could. In 1891, two ketches each brought about 100 tons of stone from St. Mawes, Cornwall, and two Irish schooners each brought 140 tons of stone from Arklow. To discharge the latter pair, Smart had to arrange seven vessel movements over six days. Further consignments of St. Mawes stone arrived in sailing vessels over the following years.

In the same period, road stone was also brought from Penmaenmawr in North Wales by a small steamer. On its first trip in December 1892, SS *Cecil* brought 185 tons for the County Council, of which 80 tons were quickly taken away by Smart's boats. The rest had to be left at Frampton Wharf, where some remained until well into the New Year because ice restricted vessel movements. The long delay in completing the delivery of the stone

THE DOCKS, SHARPNESS.

Sharpness main dock looking back towards the canal in 1905. It was common for smaller craft such as Smart's boats and barges to load here directly from larger ships.
NP

may have caused Smart some confusion, because one surviving letter from the toll clerk at the Junction answered Smart's query as to how much stone had been recorded when the steamer arrived at Sharpness.

When SS *Cecil*'s next trip was being planned to bring 200 tons, her owners wrote to Smart notifying her expected arrival date and asking him to have enough boats ready this time, as they wanted a good dispatch. Local shipping agent Victor Rowles also sent a similar request. Once again, however, the four boats Smart provided could only take away two-thirds of the cargo and the rest had to be discharged at Frampton Wharf. This prompted a rebuke from the County Surveyor, who complained that if Smart did not have enough boats available, he should not have agreed to the order being placed. When SS *Cecil* came again a year later, Smart provided four boats and a barge, and the whole cargo was discharged quickly. Other successful trips followed.

As well as collecting road stone from the Junction, James Smart's vessels also loaded large consignments of borate of lime destined for the borax factory at Inchbrook. In May 1896, two ships brought 400 tons to the Junction, and it took twelve boat and barge trips to move it to Dudbridge over the following month. The challenge of providing a quick discharge for steamers increased in 1899, when the County Council began to charter larger steamers that could carry 300 tons and seven arrived in that year. It seems that Smart rose to the challenge as no further letters of complaint have survived.

Saul Junction where the Gloucester & Sharpness Canal was crossed by the Stroudwater Canal and Stroudwater boats sometimes loaded from coastal vessels. NP

This circa 1890 photograph shows the Lancaut Quarries, on the River Wye just north of Chepstow, at the height of their production, with the whole operation crammed on to a very narrow shelf between the cliffs and the river. The stone quarried here could only be taken away by boat, so their period of operation was short, from around 1885 to 1910. Vertical-boilered steam cranes aided movement and loading at the jetties, and several wooden derricks can also be seen. CM

Chapter 5

Chepstow Stone

Smart's barges *Industry*, *Flora* and *Perseverance* regularly visited Chepstow to load limestone for the various road authorities along the Stroud Valley. At least from 1891, when records are available, the usual route was via Sharpness. The main quarries visited by Smart's barges were spread out along half a mile of cliffs on the Gloucestershire bank of the River Wye north of Chepstow Bridge at Lancaut. The cliffs had a scree at the bottom sloping down to the river, and steep tramroads and cranes were used to aid the loading of vessels. The cost of the stone depended on how much treatment it was given at the quarry. The lowest price was for rough stone, with more being charged for 'lifts' and more again for broken stone. Some stone was cut into kerbs and channelling, and very small pieces were sold as chippings or gravel. Stone for the roads needed to be broken to a fairly uniform size, such as to fit through a two inch diameter ring, but some highway authorities ordered larger cheaper blocks and then arranged to have them broken up by local men who were unemployed.

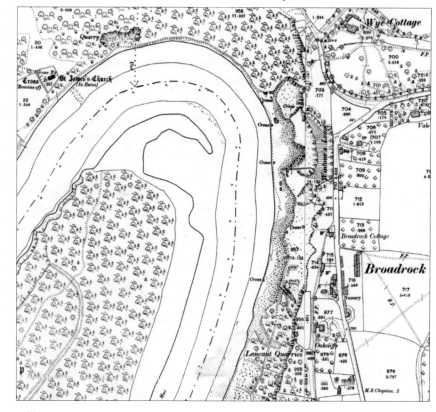

The quarries at Lancaut from the 1900 2nd Edition 25 inch OS.

James Smart carried stone for the main Chepstow quarry operators, William Jones, William Davis and John Richardson, who had contracts to supply local highway authorities and other organisations. In the 1880s, highway authorities were giving much attention to improving road surfaces, and carrying stone from Chepstow developed as a major role for Smart's barges. Most surviving letters are about Smart's dealings with Jones, although the other operators are mentioned occasionally. One letter asked Smart to send a barge to take a cargo for Stroud so they would have some stone for the men to go on breaking, adding: '*You*

*The smack **George** loading large blocks of stone at a jetty below a small quarry to the south of Chepstow bridge circa 1880. NP*

know how I am placed with the Stroud Board, and I trust you will oblige me in this matter'. Another request was more desperate: *'Please send some barges down at once. I am blocked up'*.

As well as carrying stone to the Stroud Valley, James Smart's barges also carried some loads to Bristol and to Newport. Surviving letters show that these trips were usually arranged by the barge captains themselves. One time when Henry Watkins was loading stone for Bristol, he wrote to Smart: *'Jones wants us to come back to load us for Newport'*. On another visit to Chepstow, having arrived from Newport, Watkins received a letter from Smart asking him to go to Cardiff but Watkins had other ideas. He replied: *'If I had received it at Newport, we could have got there this morning. I sent you the address where to find me there.*

The men [are] *not willing to go from here empty to Cardiff, so I got Davis* [stone merchant] *to load us for Bristol and we shall finish to leave in the morning. I hope to be at Cardiff the later part of the week'*. On a further visit in early January, intending to load stone for the Stroud Valley, Watkins heard that ice was stopping vessels moving on the Stroudwater Canal, so he wrote to Smart saying he would load for Newport instead. As he had been away from home for some time, he asked for six pounds to be sent to his wife at Saul and three days later, Mrs Watkins acknowledged receipt of the money.

Although most trips by James Smart's barges involved carrying to places along the Stroud Valley, the quarry operators sometimes wanted

*The trow **Palace** on the Wye bank at Lancaut ready to load stone in the mid 1920s.*
WA GWM 54.0646

stone taken to a riverside destination for a local highway authority. William Jones used Smart's barges to deliver stone to Minsterworth and William Davis had stone taken to The Flat in Westbury-on-Severn parish. The two men were in competition for these contracts and two letters from Davis highlight the pressure that there was to keep transport costs down. In May 1893, Davis wrote: *'The **Flora** arrived here from the Flat. I have paid the captain his freight at 2 shillings per ton. This is the same that I always paid you. But the captain says that Capt Watkins told him it was 2s 3d per ton. I don't remember ever paying him 2s 3d per ton, but if others pay it, I will do so on that cargo, but not any more as I can get plenty to carry it at 2s'*. It seems he ended up paying 2s 1d per ton and a year later, when Smart pressed for 2s 3d per ton, he wrote: *'As regards the freights on the Severn at 2s 3d per ton, this is too high as you know the prices have been cut so low I cannot afford this. I only paid to 2s 1d last year'*. He then suggested paying Smart and his captain separately, *'as we used to do'*.

Occasionally, Smart's barges carried Chepstow stone to places along the Gloucester & Sharpness Canal, including Hempsted (for roads), Monk Meadow (for building the new dock there), Gloucester timber yards (for making hard standing) and Gloucester Corporation (for roads). One cargo was loaded on to the sailing ship *Rhine* at Sharpness, presumably to serve as ballast.

Although most loads of stone were arranged in advance, it was not uncommon for a barge to turn up at a quarry on spec and take whatever stone needed delivering at that time. On one such visit, captain Alfred Meadows was stuck at Chepstow over the weekend, writing to Smart: *'We came here Friday morning. Could not find stone enough to finish* [loading] *on Saturday, sorry to say. With luck, we shall be up some time next week'*. When one of Smart's captains arrived to find that no order had been received, he agreed to carry a load that William Jones wanted delivering to the Stroud Local Board. Smart complained to Jones

Wheatenhust Union Workhouse at Eastington overlooked the Stroudwater Canal. Rough stone was delivered here to be broken by the inmates for use on local roads.

because he knew he had sent an order but Jones explained that nothing had arrived and defended what he had done.

His barges usually went to Chepstow empty, which prompted Smart to offer to start sending William Jones some Forest coal. Jones replied that he would consider some if it was cheaper than his current supply from Newport but there is no record that any was sent. One special cargo that did go to Chepstow was a steam engine used for breaking stone, that had been overhauled by Edwin Clark at Brimscombe. This followed an urgent request from Jones saying: '*I am badly in need of it as I have orders in for a cargo or two of broken stone*'.

Another letter from William Jones concerned the appropriate payment to Captain Meadows for taking 60 tons of stone from Chepstow to Bristol, as Jones had given Meadows an advance of one pound and Meadows had got away with only paying coastwise dues on 50 tons. Jones wrote: '*Please pay him as follows:* [Two] *Thirds of 60 tons @ 1s 10d, £3 10s. Coastwise dues 8s 4d. Total £3 18s 4d. Received of W Jones £1. Amount due £2 18s 4d. You will then have to charge me with 60 tons at 1s 10d and the 8s 4d coastwise dues*'. Attempting to avoid such complications, after two later trips, Jones sent a cheque direct to captain Henry Watkins for the freight charge but, unfortunately this did not help as Smart had already paid Watkins for the work.

As well as carrying stone for quarry operators, in 1891 Smart started acting as a stone merchant himself, contracting to supply highway authorities and buying stone from whichever quarry was offering it at a good price. William Davis wrote: '*I have a few cargoes of good stone ready to load and shall be glad if you will take a few cargoes out of my way. If you are having your stone cheaper, I shall be glad to know as I am prepared to supply you cheaper than anyone else will*'. Another time, he was more specific, writing: '*I should be pleased to supply you any time at 1s 4d per ton*'.

Also in 1891, James Smart arranged to have a new barge built at Bourne near Brimscombe by Matthew Gardiner. The total cost was £275, which Smart paid in instalments over the following two years. Like the earlier barges, *Excelsior* had an open hold and a single mast but with a hull breadth of 14.6 feet, she could carry up to 75 tons of cargo. The additional breadth meant that she could not pass through the locks of the Thames & Severn Canal to reach Smart's wharf at Chalford and so could only deliver as far inland as Brimscombe. After *Excelsior* came into service in September 1891, management of the old barge *Industry* passed to the Field family of Saul.

Acting as a merchant inevitably incurred additional difficulties. After James Smart complained about the quantity and loading time of one delivery, William Jones sent a long letter in response: '*Re the weight of cargo, I am willing to take your word for it and let it go at that. Now respecting the time she was here, I did it for the best. I had received your order to put that class of stone in her and began loading her the one day and finished her the next. That is the first time I have delayed beyond one day. I may also assure you that Mr Davis had not as much as one ton of broken stone in his quarry, so that the vessel could not possibly have loaded quicker anywhere else. I went through the whole of the other quarries and tried, the same day, to buy a cargo of broken stone for the Severn Bridge Rail Co, but could not buy a bit as everyone wanted more than they*

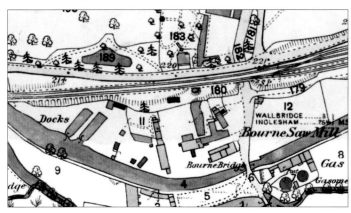

A circa 1908 view looking down on the Gardiner's boat yard, behind the tree in the left foregound, with the Thames & Severn Canal snaking past Bourne Mill and the gas works, and with Brimscombe station in the right background. The boat yard was where several of James Smart's boats and barges were built and maintained, and is shown on the 1885 25 inch OS extract, left, as twin dry docks. NP

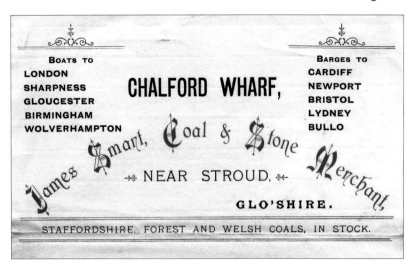

Letterheading used by Smart from 1894, when he became a stone merchant as well as dealing in coal. GA D4367/2/2 C53

Stone piled beside Chalford round house with Smart's house in the background. MM

had got. I then turned to and broke [stone for you] *and got it on board – so you can see for yourself I did my very best for you'.*

Most consignments of stone were ordered in advance, so the right quality would be ready when the barge arrived but communication difficulties could upset careful plans. After William Jones had prepared good quality 'lifts' so he could load *Flora* away on a tide, he was upset to see her pass by to John Richardson's quarry and load for him. Jones wrote to Smart saying: *'I have had to put the* [good quality] *stone in the* **Dora** *today as rough stone. So I leave you to judge what inconvenience your captain has this day put me to. If this is being done with your permission, I may say I am sorry you did not let me know she was not to load lifts. If it is done without your knowledge or permission, it is a pity such a man should sail the vessel'.*

As well as James Smart acting as a stone merchant, which involved him paying the quarry operators, he also continued to carry stone for the operators for which they had to pay him. Over the course of a year, the receipts from and payments to a given quarry operator tended to balance out, so it was only occasionally necessary for money to change hands. So when Smart was short of funds and pressed William Jones to settle his account, Jones replied reluctantly: *'I will endeavour to send you a cheque the latter part of this week. You seem to blame me for this account – had you sent the vessels here, I should have wiped the account out by now as you know'.*

When Smart had more business for his barges than he could manage, he could usually call on another owner to help out but on one such occasion, arrangements went badly wrong. When approached by Smart, Zaccheus Whiting of Eastington was happy to agree to the use of his barge **Wherry Packet** and he wrote to his captain George Clark asking him to agree details with Smart. Whiting had also received a request for help from James Herbert, to meet his vessel **John** at the Junction and deliver her cargo of coal to the Stroud Gas Company but he was under the impression

THE JUNCTION SAUL.

*The schooner **Julia** of Gloucester moored beside the boatyard at Saul Junction circa 1900. Men are fitting a new topsail and others are applying metal sheeting to protect the hull when the anchor was lifted aboard. NP*

that this was not imminent. Unfortunately, however, *John* arrived at the Junction before Clark had made arrangements with Smart and so Smart was left without the help he wanted. Trying to be helpful, Whiting wrote: '*Although I want to send her to Bullo when this is done, if its not too late, I will put off the Bullo voyage, and she shall go at once for you. I am very sorry – I hope it will never occur again. Kindly write if its not too late and I will do my best to oblige you*'.

In 1893, a quarry near Chepstow formerly run by Elizabeth Rowles of Frampton on Severn was taken over by William Davis and he wrote to James Smart offering to supply stone from there: '*I am certain you will get better stone from me than any other merchant at Chepstow. I am prepared to supply you cheaper than anyone else can and shall be pleased to meet you any day to arrange matters*'. Having recently talked with William Jones and perhaps not getting a satisfactory response, Smart invited Davis to Chalford and in due course agreed to take up his offer. Davis wrote: '*Thanks for the promise of your barges. I take it that you will give me all your stone orders at that price. I have some good stone at Rowles old quarry, and your barges can continue carrying from there*'.

When a barge was leaving Chepstow, it was common for the captain to send Smart an expected arrival time, so he could make arrangements for discharging the cargo. Sometimes the captain needed to ask where to deliver. From Chepstow, Watkins wrote: '*We shall get our stone to leave here tomorrow morning, hoping to be in the Point Friday. Please leave orders at Stroud where to discharge the stone*'. In another letter from Chepstow, Watkins wrote: '*Jones*

*Rough and broken stone on the wharf at Brimscombe, with James Smart's barge **Gem** alongside.*
GA GPS 609/18

wants this cargo at Stroud. I have not said anything to him about you wanting it [at Chalford]. *If you intend him to have it, let me know by wire tomorrow night at Saul.'*

Before barges left Chepstow, requests were sometimes sent to Smart asking for a donkey to be available for the return trip along the Stroudwater Canal. When two barges were about to leave, stone merchant William Jones asked Smart to send donkeys to the Junction. On a subsequent visit, Henry Watkins asked for *'a donkey'* and on a different visit Alfred Meadows asked for *'another donkey'*. These words could indicate that one donkey had been used to tow each empty barge on the outward voyage and, as this had been left at Saul Junction, a second donkey was needed to tow the loaded barge back up the canal. It is unfortunate that there are no other references to how donkeys were managed.

As most of James Smart's barge crews came from the villages near to the Severn, it was understood that returning barges would stop for a night or more in that area, particularly at a weekend, and this was an opportunity to send and receive letters. When returning from one trip, Charles Matthews arrived at the Junction at midday on a Friday, and he managed

Road stone piled on the County Council's stone wharf along the pound above Chalford Chapel Lock circa 1912. The donkey and lad were engaged on bread deliveries around the village. HB

to stay there two and a half days as he heard that there was a stoppage on the canal up to Stroud. After arriving at the Junction with stone from Chepstow, Watkins wrote: '*Your letter this morning did not give me any instructions what to do when empty. Are we to go to Newport from here. If so the coal must be ordered for Thursday. Please send me five pounds*'. Having suffered heavy weather, George Everett reported a delay due to a broken chain and a split staysail, both of which he had repaired, and he hoped to get away soon. He continued: '*There is one thing I want – that is a compass. The one I have there is no use. It may lead me to loose ship and ourselves. It is not worth repairing or I should have taken it to Bristol. Please try to get one*'.

Usually Smart's barges discharged at one of the wharfs along the Stroudwater and Thames & Severn canals as far as Chalford but sometimes he arranged for all or part of the cargo to be transshipped at or near Saul Junction. This could be necessary if a barge was required to go on another trip urgently, perhaps to load at Bullo on a spring tide. Also, it was sometimes necessary to lighten a large barge like *Excelsior* to reduce its draft and so allow it to be towed up the Stroudwater Canal more easily. The preferred practice was to transfer the cargo from barge to narrowboat while both were moored in the basin at the Junction. Alternatively, if all of Smart's narrowboats were busy, the cargo could be discharged at Frampton Wharf on the Sharpness Canal or alongside Whitminster Lock on the Stroudwater Canal, from where it was collected later when boats became available.

Anticipating the need for such a discharge for *Excelsior*, Henry Watkins wrote from

Two donkeys pulling a heavy barge at Lodgemore Bridge on the Stroudwater Canal. MM

Chepstow: *'We have load today and hope to be in the Point* [Sharpness] *tomorrow morning. If the boats is not there* [at the Junction] *waiting, send them as soon on Monday morning as you can'*. When he needed another such discharge, Smart only had one boat available and Watkins wrote: *'We have loaded the boat and I shall put the remainder on the Shallow Lock side* [Whitminster Lock]. *There will be 35 tons there. If the coal is not ordered* [at Bullo], *please do so at once, as we have to be there to load Monday if all is well'*. As there would not be time for him to get to Chalford to collect his wages, he added: *'Please send me seven pounds to Saul by return'*.

When passing up the Stroudwater Canal, a heavily loaded barge could have difficulty navigating the pound above Whitminster Lock. If the Sharpness Canal was at its full level, the lock served little purpose and the gates were not needed, so were not properly maintained. However, when the tidal basin at Sharpness had to be used as a lock by ships that were too big to fit in the normal lock, there was a noticable reduction in the level of the ship canal and hence of the connected length of the Stroudwater Canal. In July 1896, when the water level was 10 inches down, *Excelsior* took four hours from Saul Junction to Whitminster Lock and another four hours from there to Bristol Road Lock. Going the other way loaded with gravel in November 1895, *Excelsior* took seven and a half hours to go from Bristol Road Lock just over a mile to Whitminster Lock with one horse and six donkeys, and also needing the use of a windlass to get it out of the tail of the upper lock. These difficulties rumbled on for several years until eventually Whitminster Lock was made operable again.

Even if there was adequate water in the canal, it was hard work for two donkeys to pull a fully laden stone barge and occasionally one incurred an injury, which if not treated could lead to a charge of cruelty to animals. In one case, a donkey was found to have two large open wounds on the left shoulder and crewman Herbert Boucher admitted that unless a man had a strong stomach, the sight was enough to knock him down. Boucher was fined 5s, his captain Henry Meadows £2 and owner James Smart £3, all with costs. If a barge stopped anywhere en route, the crew were expected to prevent the donkeys from straying and when captain Henry Ralph did not do this, he was fined 5s.

Chapter 6

Bristol Channel Ports

During the 1880s and '90s, James Smart's barges made regular trips to ports in the Bristol Channel, such as Bristol, Avonmouth, Newport and occasionally Cardiff. They could not go further afield because each had an open hold and so were restricted by Board of Trade regulations to the area of relatively sheltered water referred to as 'East of the Holms' – the islands of Steep Holm and Flat Holm in the Bristol Channel. While not being as exposed as the open sea, these waters were nevertheless subject to very strong tidal flows and unpredictable weather conditions, and so Smart recruited his crews from the families of experienced local mariners who lived in villages such as Frampton on Severn, Saul and Fretherne. As mentioned previously, from 1891 at least – when records are available – the usual route to and from the Bristol Channel was via Sharpness.

In the 1880s, the barges frequently made trips to Bristol or Avonmouth to collect grain, timber, sticks or road stone for destinations in the Stroud Valley. The grain and timber were evidently imports and many cargoes were loaded overside from ships, although some timber consignments came from merchants' stock. For the outward voyage, most barges

Bristol floating harbour looking north towards the drawbridge in 1880.
BA 43207/17/1

~ 59 ~

The Avon Gorge in 1877, with quarries on both sides of the river. A steam barge is loading at the jetty on the right and several other small craft are in the Avon. NP

were empty but there were occasional cargoes of flour and converted timber from mills in the Stroud Valley, and in the early days Smart also arranged for some cargoes of grain, timber and salt to be loaded at Gloucester.

The sticks loaded at Bristol were on their way to factories in the Stroud Valley that made walking sticks and umbrellas. They usually came as small consignments discharged direct from ships and at least one such consignment of 30 tons of turned wood valued at £500 was insured for the voyage from Bristol to Sharpness. To fill the rest of the space in the hold, it was usual to load road stone from one of the quarries in the Avon Gorge or in the Wye Valley.

At least one load of sticks apparently from Bristol was not imported. John Rudge and the barge *Industry* were recorded returning to the Stroudwater Canal on 1st October 1886 with 45 tons of sticks from Bristol, having left the canal for Bristol five weeks earlier. However, a letter to Smart, just dated September 1886, shows that from Bristol he had travelled up the Kennet & Avon Canal to the Thames and loaded the sticks near Reading. He said he would hire a horse to help get to Newbury (against the flow in the River Kennet), then continue with the donkey alone and he would write again from Bath asking for a boy to be sent by train to meet him at Bristol, to bring the donkey back to Chalford.

Smart's barges also regularly visited Newport, to load smith's coal destined for various foundries along the line of the Stroudwater and Thames & Severn canals. They collected shipments from the Powell, Duffryn Steam Coal Co. and Henry Powell's Aberbeeg Colliery, and Smart also had occasional truck loads sent to Brimscombe station, presumably when a small quantity of smith's coal was required urgently.

The barges also went frequently to Newport to load superphosphate 'manure', which was sent by the manufacturing chemists Morris & Griffin Ltd to destinations along the Stroudwater and Thames & Severn canals. Unfortunately, the company was not happy with one invoice submitted by Smart and when he pressed for payment, he received a

Morris & Griffin letterhead from 1893. MiP 2008.74/52

The docks and the coal staithes along the River Usk at Newport. NP

A close-up of one of the riverside staithes at Newport, with the transporter bridge in the background. Used for loading smaller coastal trading vessels, Smart's barges would have loaded coal at these drops. NP

letter blaming him for inaccurate information sent earlier, adding: '*As a businessman, you know accounts must be checked before being paid. It will afford us as much pleasure as you when all is in order between us*'. It took several more letters from Newport and from the company's head office in Wolverhampton to get the matter clarified.

A different traffic emanated from Newport in 1887, when Smart's barges made about a dozen trips to collect tree trunks from a local estate, for delivery to Dudbridge for timber merchant Henry Workman, who had a steam saw mill at Woodchester. Initially, the haulier delivered so many logs to the dockside in Newport that he blocked the space there, so Workman wrote asking Smart to send a vessel immediately and to say when it was expected to arrive, so he could notify the haulier and the wharfinger accordingly.

James Smart's barges occasionally visited Cardiff to load coal for the Stroud Valley, for which Smart had dealings with Cory Brothers & Co. On one visit, *Flora* was held up in the tidal basin at the entrance to one of the Bute Docks, because there was a shortage of water in the dock and the entrance gates were kept closed until tide time. On another visit, when due to load in the Ely River, captain Henry Watkins wrote: '*I have seen Cory Brothers and they have promised to load us tomorrow morning. If the weather permits, we shall have tomorrow day tide*'. However, when Smart inquired about regularly loading 150 to 200 tons a month, Cory Brothers wrote: '*We can only ship at Ely Harbour on the understanding that you pay us 6d a ton more than Cardiff or Barry prices as we make the screenings at Cardiff and Barry, and it would cost us 6d a ton to transfer them to Ely Harbour from those places*'. One unusual cargo from Cardiff was 30 tons of sand in barrels and some moss litter (for bedding horses), whilst a rare cargo to Cardiff comprised 30 tons of cider from Ebley.

As well as regularly visiting the ports mentioned above, Smart's barges occasionally called at Bridgwater to load tiles, pipes and bricks, and at Brockweir and Oldbury to load timber. A barge even visited Caerleon and Newbridge on the River Usk, to load a cargo from wood hoop and timber merchant Henry Lewis. Barges also carried coal from Bullo Pill to Lympsham up the River Axe in Somerset.

To be able to manage the wide ranging movements of his barges, Smart relied heavily on frequent progress reports from his captains. Some letters just reported the discharge of a cargo or gave a reason for being delayed but others also said where the barge was going next or asked for orders. On one visit to Bristol, Henry Watkins reported that he was delayed because rain had stopped the men from work but he hoped to leave the following night. On another visit, Watkins wrote: '*We are load and shall leave here tonight, hoping to be at the Point [i.e. Sharpness Point] tomorrow and at Stroud Monday*'. Again from Bristol, Henry Watkins wrote: '*Hope to discharge Monday. Please send orders what we are to do when empty*'. Also from Bristol, Charles Matthews wrote that he had had to put on extra men to get some sticks loaded as there was a steam boat in the way, adding that the loading of some fertiliser had run over into a second day.

Several letters from Smart's captains highlighted the difficulties of being available at the

Coal staithes at Ely Harbour, Cardiff. JN

*The inner lock entrance to Bute West Dock, Cardiff, as seen from the top of the Dock Offices circa 1910. Bottom left is part of the tidal basin where **Flora** was held up due to a shortage of water in the dock on one visit. NP*

right time to receive a consignment being discharged overside from a ship – arriving late could mean losing the cargo to railway transport and a hurried rearrangement of future plans. In one letter, Henry Watkins explained that while crossing from Cardiff to Bristol, he had had to beat against a strong wind and although he had come to Bristol as soon as he could, he found the wheat he was due to collect had already gone by rail. As he could find no other cargo, he proposed to go to Chepstow and load stone for the Stroud Valley. On another visit to Bristol, Watkins reported that by the time his cargo to Bristol was discharged, it would be too late to collect the 400 sacks of wheat he was due to load, as the ship would have finished discharging. This was also reported to the customer in Stroud, who had the wheat sent on by rail. This time Smart hurriedly arranged for the barge to collect some round timber from Newport before returning home.

Other letters reported delays due to the late arrival of a ship or missing paperwork. John Rudge wrote that the steamer he was due to load from had only arrived that morning

Bristol City Docks circa 1905, looking east along the floating harbour, with Canon's Marsh Wharf on the left and Princes's Wharf straight ahead. NP

and he did not expect that his timber would be got out until the following day. Another time, Rudge wrote that he had taken in 100 sacks of barley but had not received orders concerning two other expected consignments. The relevant customers had been contacted by telegram on Saturday but as no replies had been received, he would have to wait there until Monday. Rudge was held up again when a lack of paperwork delayed the release of 170 cases of sticks brought from New York by the SS *Devon*.

When there were delays, some letters asked for money to be sent to cover living and vessel operating expenses. From Bristol, Alfred Meadows explained that he was waiting for his cargo to be discharged from a ship and he asked for one pound to be sent to H.R. James' office, Queen Square. New captain Alfred Meadows was also held up because he was not aware that agent W.K. Harris acted for Smart in dealing with customs matters and as he had been away from home for some time, he asked Smart to send one pound by return of post for living expenses.

Hilly Orchard Bridge on the Stroudwater Canal, with the trow **Gertrude** *which regularly traded to Bristol in competition with James Smart's barges. It is likely the sails were raised just for the photograph. HB*

A view down the Stroud Valley from above Brimscombe circa 1908, showing some of the mills served by James Smart with the Thames & Severn Canal and the railway running parallel along the contours of the hillside. On the right is Ham Mill, in the centre distance is Stafford Mill and between them is Griffin's Mill. NP

When difficulties arose, it was sometimes the captain who decided what action to take. As the captain and crew were paid per cargo, they did not like waiting for a ship to arrive or travelling empty between ports. When Henry Watkins found he would have to wait four days at Bristol for a ship bringing some sticks, he knew there would be another barge visiting Bristol soon and so he decided to go to Chepstow and load stone. Although Watkins made some decisions to suit himself, he was also conscious of the need to fulfil commitments or business could be lost to the railways. When he arrived late at Avonmouth to receive 700 sacks of wheat from a ship, he initially could not find out anything about the expected cargo but he did not give up. By making further inquiries, he was able to establish that, although some had been sent on by rail, he was still able to load 460 sacks.

With so much activity happening over a wide area, it was inevitable that James Smart occasionally lost track of what was going on and that some messages sent did not reach their intended destination. When one barge did not arrive at Newport to load coal as expected, agent W.K. Harris wrote in frustration: '*I do not know what the end will be. All the cargo was got to the berth for shipping. You do not say where she is or if she is about going for the coal*'.

By the start of 1893, Smart's barges were maintaining a busy schedule but competition from the railways kept freight charges low and during the winter of 1892-93, he got behind with paying his bills. One example concerned the Powell, Duffryn Steam Coal Co. at Newport, who wrote in January seeking settlement for coal supplied in October and getting no response, they wrote again in February. Smart did send money this time but he deducted the usual $2^1/_2\%$ discount for prompt payment, with the company then having to point out that it was not allowable in this case.

In February 1893, James Smart heard about a possible new line of business carrying manganese ore from Newport to S.G. Bailey & Co's mill near Stroud for use in making paint – but the enterprise started badly. As the first consignment of ore was only 30 tons, Smart also ordered about 25 tons of coal from Powell, Duffryn & Co. to fill the barge. However, when captain Alfred Meadows arrived in *Flora*, he found himself in difficulties. On 13th March, he wrote to Smart saying: *'The coal is here ready but I can't find out anything about the ore. The ship is in the Alexandra Dock finished discharging yesterday. I shall have to find her broker tomorrow before I can know anything'*. Two days later, as Meadows had still not made contact, Bailey & Co. sent Smart a telegram *'Where is barge Wire urgent'* – but it was too late and the following day the shipping agent reported that, as they had not heard news of the barge, Bailey & Co. had authorised the manganese ore be sent by rail.

Meadows then went to load the coal that Smart had ordered but it was only half a load. So on 20th March, he sent Smart a telegram: *'Flora shipped 30 tons. Wire orders Powell's office immediate'*. Smart initially asked him to go to Cardiff by train to see about a cargo of rags that had just arrived but as this came to nothing, he did authorise the extra coal. Smart evidently blamed Meadows for the loss of the new cargo opportunity and he immediately wrote asking Charles Matthews to take over as captain of *Flora*. However, the incident did not cause lasting damage and many cargoes of manganese ore were carried successfully over the following years.

Also in February 1893, Smart heard of another new line of business, involving the movement of rags in bales from Cardiff to the Stroud area. He was invited to quote for carrying 150 tons of rags for the whole distance in one barge if that was practical or, if necessary, just from Framilode along the Stroudwater Canal to Stroud. Smart arranged for Henry Watkins to make enquiries when on a visit to Cardiff and he reported that the rags were bulky and a barge could only carry 30 tons (rather than 60 tons for a cargo like coal).

Sailing ships and floating timber in Alexandra Dock Newport circa 1900. NP

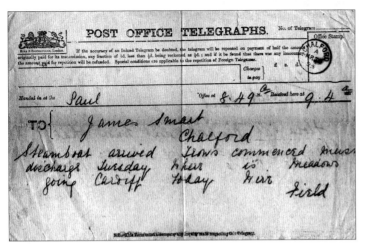

Telegram sent by Hubert Field on 20th March 1893 before setting off to Cardiff to supervise transshipment of a consignment of rags. GA D4367/2/2 C22

Smart agreed terms with the agents in Cardiff and he involved fellow carrier Hubert Field, who also had a vessel that could load at the South Wales port

On the day the steamer was due (20th March), Field went to Cardiff to finalise arrangements and there he joined up with Alfred Meadows, who had been sent by Smart just after the manganese ore fiasco. On the following day, Field reported in disgust that there were only 75 tons or so to go to the Stroud area and that, by the time he arrived, transshipment into two locally arranged vessels had already started. Meadows had told him that *Flora* was half loaded with coal at Newport and therefore would not be of much use even if she did come the following day, for if she had replaced the second vessel, she could not have taken all of what the first had left. He went on: '*I don't know what arrangements you made about quantities, but I consider we have been humbugged over the job*'. As the two vessels being loaded would be too big to pass up the Stroudwater Canal, he finished by saying his barges would be ready to meet them at Saul Junction if Smart's were not available.

Bristol City Docks, a view looking east from Prince Street swing bridge circa 1905. Note the barge loaded with timber on the right. NP

When the two vessels arrived at the Junction, they were met by a boat and a barge from Smart and two barges from Field, and the rags were duly delivered to shoddy makers in Brimscombe and Dudbridge to be shredded and recycled. However, Smart's first invoice for this service was rejected by the Cardiff agents as, to allow for the help provided by Field, he charged a higher rate per ton than he had quoted initially. The agents insisted that they had nothing whatever to do with Field and Smart had to reduce his charge to the original quote. When another consignment of rags was expected, Smart quoted the higher rate and asked for the option of sending barges when available but the agents wanted to have the barges on a fixed date for discharging overside and so no agreement was possible.

Jones & Wainwright letterhead dated 1894. GA D4367/2/2 C50

While all this was going on, Smart also came under pressure to take on carrying small consignments between Stroud and Bristol. For many years, a regular service had been in the hands of William Knee but that business was declining – at the start of 1893, the frequency of trips reduced from twice to once a month. Concerned that traffic was being lost to the railways, the manager of the Stroudwater Navigation Company, W.J. Snape, wrote to Smart saying that grocers in Stroud were making enquiries as to having Bristol goods by water but no one called on them. He added that the railway people were always going about seeking business and he suggested that Smart should have circulars printed and left at the shops. Smart was not keen on the idea and when Knee offered to sell his trow *Sea Breeze* and the goodwill of the business for £250, he did not take up the offer. He evidently recognised that the days of running a regular service by water were over.

As it became clear that William Knee was going to give up running *Sea Breeze* in early 1894, his Bristol agent W.K. Harris tried to transfer some of his business to James Smart. When timber merchants Jones & Wainwright had two large consignments to send to Bowbridge and Dudbridge, Harris wrote to Smart: '*I gave Jones & Wainwright your name and address which accounts for them writing you. I claim the usual commission 2$^{1}/_{2}$ per cent on freight (not canal dues). The captain of **Sea Breeze** says the rate has been 5s in full, but you must understand these are not fir deals but beach, and I shall agree at 5s per load of 3 tons the standard not 2$^{1}/_{2}$ as fir deals. Am I to act for the future for you or not? Knee paid me 2s 6d each voyage and you can do the same, only let me know yes or no*'. Recognising that he might have appeared to be betraying a confidence, he was no doubt pleased to write on the following day: '*The **Sea Breeze** is sold. So the road is quite clear for us to act properly. I expect to be at Stroud next week. Can we meet*'. With the vessel sold, Smart did agree to take over Knee's residual business and *Flora* did carry the two consignments but it did not lead to much further business. The next consignment Jones & Wainwright wanted carrying to a builder in Paganhill was only 3 tons and this alone was not worth Smart sending a barge for.

Meanwhile, in April 1893, captain Henry Watkins had received a letter from James Smart about another new line of business – carrying wheat from Bristol to Stratford Flour Mills, Stroud, for millers Kemble & Dash. Having made inquiries at Bristol, Watkins wrote back to Smart saying that the first cargo comprised 50 tons of flour and 22 tons of wheat, for which the bags were expected in the morning. As the flour and wheat needed protection in the open hold of *Excelsior*, Watkins hired three canvas cloths from Thomas & Hyatt, ship chandlers & sail makers, and the vessel returned to the Stroudwater Canal on 10th April.

For the next cargo for Stratford Mill, Henry Watkins and *Excelsior* arrived at Bristol on 18th April only to find that the ship bringing the wheat would not arrive for six days. Also, he could not find anyone who knew about the wheat, as it had been ordered through Weston Hewletts of Gloucester,

Kemble & Dash letterhead dated 1892. MiP 2008.74/34

R. Townsend & Co. Ltd bought Stratford Mill from Kemble & Dash in 1901. Seen here after a fire in 1908, it was rebuilt and Townsends continued in business. HB

Avonmouth Docks.

Avonmouth Docks circa 1900, where Smart's barges loaded. NP

who had no office in Bristol. He asked Smart to see to the necessary paperwork or he feared being delayed even longer. Eventually, 60 tons of wheat were loaded and *Excelsior* returned to the Stroudwater Canal on 2nd May.

For the third cargo for Stratford Mill, Kemble & Dash reported that the steamer with 500 sacks of wheat for them had gone to Avonmouth, instead of Bristol as had been expected. Fortunately, *Flora* was discharging a previous cargo at Avonmouth and Smart was able to notify captain Charles Matthews that he did not have to go to Bristol after all. However, Matthews found he could not collect the wheat immediately because the bags had been sent to Bristol. Having asked for them to be forwarded, he wrote to Smart: '*If they come tonight, we may get loaded tomorrow, but if not, they will load other vessels out of their turn before us*'. Fortunately, all went well and *Flora* soon returned to the Stroudwater Canal, and after these teething difficulties, carrying wheat to Stratford Mill became routine business for Smart's barges.

A view of the River Severn from Newnham circa 1910, showing the vast sandbanks which reduced the width of the navigable channel on the way from the Stroudwater Canal to Bullo Dock, which is just behind the white building in the centre right distance. The riverside deepwater wharf at Box Meadow can be seen in the left distance but was out of use by this date and the tips removed. NP

Chapter 7

Sea Mills and More

In March 1891, James Smart's barges were given a new trading opportunity, carrying coal from Bullo Dock to Thomas Sharpe at Sea Mills on the Avon, north-west of Bristol. Amos Field of Saul, an old friend, wrote suggesting that Smart should call to see him to discuss taking over the contract, together with the planks and baskets he had used for discharging, and to agree a payment for the goodwill of the business. Field added: '*Also if you come, I thought to ask you to bring me a couple of good walking sticks in return for my anchor Capt Watkins lost some time back*'. A few days later, Smart received a letter from Sharpe asking for a vessel

to be sent to Bullo to load coal and to bring it to his wharf just after the top of the spring tides. Sharpe expected that the freight charge would be the same as he had paid Field, expressing a preference for sending a cheque related to the bill of lading rather than paying the captain. Evidently these terms were agreed, as Sharpe later sent a cheque paying for $61^1/_2$ tons carried by **Flora** at the specified rate. This new agreement with Thomas Sharpe provided the welcome prospect of regular down-river cargoes, whilst an added bonus was that he also wanted occasional cargoes of coal carried from South Wales ports to Avonmouth, where he had a contract for supplying a dozen engines.

The agreement with Thomas Sharpe soon provided good business for Smart's barges but this new trade required more complex management. Barges could only access Bullo Dock for a few days each month around the time of the spring tides, and so other trips needed to be fitted in around this. As Sharpe also wanted coal carried from

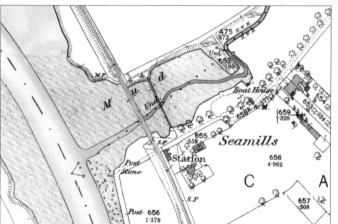

Sea Mills harbour, with the entrance off the River Avon beneath the railway bridge. The map extract left, from the 1889 1st edition 25 inch OS, shows the extent of what in the 18th century had been a wet dock.

~ 73 ~

Newport or Cardiff to Avonmouth when needed, crews could be away from home for longer than when just doing the out and back trips that they were used to. Furthermore, if William Jones of Chepstow also wanted a cargo of stone taken to Bristol or South Wales, a barge might be kept busy for a month or more before it returned home. In managing these voyages, James Smart received many letters and telegrams from his captains and his customers.

A particular topic for letters concerned the arrangements that needed to be made to order coal to be sent by rail to Bullo Dock at a time when a barge could be there to collect it. An added complication was that Sharpe placed some of his orders through coal factor Lewellin Twining. Well before one trip, Sharpe wrote to Smart: *'I shall want a cargo this spring I expect. Please let me know when **Flora** can load so that I can order coal. I do not yet know what colliery we shall order from'*. On another occasion, Twining wrote: *'Kindly let us know whether you are sending the **Excelsior** or the **Flora** for Mr Sharpe's coal, and to save time, you should send a postcard also to the Foxes Bridge Colliery telling them when the vessel will be at Bullo'*. Prior to another voyage, Sharpe wrote: *'Re your wire, I have sent same to Mr Twining asking him to let you know where and when coal will be ready for you'*. Another time, after the coal had been ordered, Sharpe confirmed: *'I have ordered coal for Tuesday, Bullo'*. Inevitably, matters did not always go according to plan and there were occasions when a barge arrived at Bullo only to find that no coal was available. After one such instance was reported by Smart, Sharpe replied: *'The coal was ordered last Friday. I have not heard anything since, but will write them again tonight and ask them to get her loaded'*.

Many other letters concerned arrangements for other business for the barges, which had to fit in with the trips from Bullo to Sea Mills around the time of the spring tides. From Bullo Dock, Watkins wrote that he hoped to be at Sea Mills to discharge on Saturday and he reminded Smart to write to Cardiff asking for his next cargo of coal to be ready on Monday. On the way from Bullo to Sea Mills, Alfred Meadows stopped for the weekend at Brickhills, on the south side of the Arlingham peninsula, and walked home to Epney. While there he wrote suggesting that if Smart was going to Gloucester Market, he could send any instructions via the carrier John Knight, who could be contacted at the Talbot

Foxes Bridge Colliery circa 1904. Coal was supplied to Bullo via the GWR from Bilson, to which wagons were lowered by the rope-worked incline crossing the main lines in the foreground. NP

Nr. Cinderford.   Foxes Bridge Colliery.

Inn. Before leaving Chepstow for Newport, Watkins wrote: '*If Mr Sharp wants any coal this spring* [tide] *let me know at Newport. Liverpool Wharf will find me*'. Inevitably, some messages did not reach their intended recipient. At Sea Mills, a postcard addressed to Charles Matthews '*c/o Mr Sharpe, the coal merchant*' only arrived after the captain had left and it was sent back to Smart marked '*Returned to sender*'.

Some voyages were delayed by strong winds and many messages quoting an expected arrival date included the proviso '*if weather permits*'. On a visit to Cardiff, Henry Watkins reported: '*We are loaded and shall leave here in the morning if weather permits for us. I should have left tonight but it is blowing hard from the westward, but I hope it will be better in the morning*'. When *Flora* was overdue at Sea Mills, coal merchant Thomas Sharpe wrote: '*I hope the **Flora** will soon get here as we have been out of coal for a week. I suppose it was owing to the weather she could not get down, as I understand she was loaded* [ten days ago]. *It is now very bad weather and without an alteration she will not get down this week again*'.

Smart's captains also played a role in arranging future business, particularly as they were in direct contact with regular customers such as William Jones at Chepstow, and Thomas

*The brigantine **Lynwood** being towed out of the Bute West Dock Basin, Cardiff, while a trow is moored waiting to enter. SR*

Sharpe at Sea Mills and Avonmouth. Several letters included reports such as: *'We are discharging today and shall leave here tonight for Cardiff to load for Sharpe as the coal is badly wanted'*. And when Watkins heard from Sharpe that there was an urgent need to order coal to be ready for collection from Bullo Dock, he personally called on coal factor Twining to order the coal from the colliery.

Another topic for letters concerned the settlement of customers' accounts. For dealings with Thomas Sharpe, the main item was the freight charge for the carriage of particular cargoes of coal from Bullo Dock to Sea Mills and/or from South Wales to Avonmouth but a settlement also had to take account of items such as an advance to a captain or a correction to a previous account. Each captain would leave home with enough cash to cover living and vessel running expenses for the expected time away but if the trip was extended, he could apply to Sharpe for an advance that would be deducted from the freight charge at the time of settlement. In response to one account from Smart, Thomas Sharpe wrote claiming four pounds for an advance to the captain on the cargo concerned and an extra pound for a last minute advance on the previous cargo, that Sharpe had only learned about after the previous settlement. In response to another account for two cargoes, Sharpe wrote claiming advances of two pounds paid to the captain for each trip and an overcharge for two tons from a previous trip.

James Smart also received letters concerned with settling accounts with his captains, particularly if they had not returned to Chalford for an extended period. The main item was the payment to a captain of an agreed fraction of each freight charge (one third being common), plus any expenses the captain had paid out, less any advances the captain had received. Working out the net payment could involve complex multiplication as well as simple addition and subtraction. On one occasion, George Everett wrote from Bullo: *'The last freight was 61 tons* [in addition to 60 tons being loaded], *and the money I have drawn on account is £7 from Sharpe and £3 from you. The carrier's money* [for bringing the coal to the dock] *comes to £3 10s 7d at 7d per ton. The two freights at 2s 7d per ton come to £15 12s 7d. My expenses is 15s Bristol dues and 10s Bullo dues. Would you please send me balance for these two freights by postal order'*.

In January 1893, Thomas Sharpe was particularly keen for *Excelsior* to go to Cardiff to load for Avonmouth and he wrote to James Smart emphasising that the coal was wanted by Thursday next, as there was a great possibility of a strike in Wales the following week. Two days later, however, Sharpe learned that *Excelsior* had passed up the Avon with a cargo for Bristol and he wrote to Smart expressing his frustration. He complained bitterly about being misled all week, describing Smart's transactions as unbusinesslike and adding that he was obliged to telegram for a load of coal to be sent by rail, for which he thought Smart ought to pay the difference. Two more days later, Sharpe wrote again saying he still had not heard any news of *Excelsior*: '*We are out of coal at Avonmouth and very short at Sea Mills. If* [the captain] *does not think it worth while to let me know whether he intends to go or not, I certainly must get another vessel. There are about a dozen engines and 200 men which would be stopped in consequence of no coal, which is not a thing to be played with*'. It seems that Sharpe eventually received his deliveries as business returned to normal.

A circa 1900 view from the top of the cliffs at Lancaut, with a pair of barges sat on the mud loading stone whilst another waits its turn in the river. NP

3/666. J.V.   (7). TIDENHAM BEND, CHEPSTOW.

Transporter Bridge — *Newport. Mon.*

A view up river on the Usk through the transporter bridge, showing the coal staithes on the Newport bank on the left where Smart's barges loaded. NP

Two months later, however, Henry Watkins was getting into difficulties trying to juggle the requirements of regular customers William Jones and Thomas Sharpe. While at Chepstow loading stone for Bristol, Watkins was asked by Jones to bring *Excelsior* straight back to carry stone to Newport. As this meant he would not be able to collect the next load of coal from Bullo for Sharpe at Sea Mills, Watkins asked Smart if *Flora* could do this trip instead. He also asked for six pounds to be sent to his wife for her to share with the crew's wives. Unfortunately, as Alfred Meadows was busy at Newport and Cardiff, *Flora* could not be spared to load at Bullo and so Sharpe had to miss a delivery. To make matters worse, when *Excelsior* returned to Chepstow, she was just too late to load stone on Saturday as expected and so had to wait until Monday. This meant that when she eventually reached Newport, Watkins found there was not enough water in the River Usk for her to get into the berth to discharge and he had to take the cargo to Avonmouth instead. At Avonmouth, Sharpe asked Watkins to collect coal from Cardiff. By the time he returned to Avonmouth and discharged, Sharpe was desperate for coal at Sea Mills, so Watkins knew he would have to go direct to Bullo empty instead of going up river with Chepstow stone for the Stroud Valley as usual.

He wrote to Smart: 'We shall have to load before Friday next or we shan't get any coal this spring [tide], and they are nearly out at Sea Mills. I have seen Sharpe today and have promised him to go for him, and he has ordered the coal for us'. As he had been away for such a long time, Watkins promised to visit Chalford while *Excelsior* was at Bullo.

During the following month, there was further confusion concerning the supply of coal to Avonmouth for Thomas Sharpe. At the beginning of April, Sharpe asked James Smart to provide a vessel to go to Cardiff at once, expecting that Watkins would oblige as had been arranged earlier. Watkins initially said he would not be able to go before the end of the following week but later sent a message saying he could go earlier after all. However, by then Sharpe had arranged for a Bristol vessel to do the trip and he complained that Watkins' changes of mind were very provoking. Two months later, Sharpe expressed his concern again, writing to Smart: 'Will you inform me where the *Excelsior* is likely to be as I want a cargo of coal to Avonmouth and I expected to hear from the captain before this'.

It was evidently proving difficult for Smart to give Sharpe the reliable service he needed and at the end of June, Sharpe wrote to say that his customers at Avonmouth had decided to have the coal in future by rail instead of by water. Recognising that *Excelsior* was due to be at Cardiff specially, he offered to try to get her one last load if the strong wind did not prevent her going but three days later he wrote again saying it was now too late for *Excelsior* to load coal at Cardiff, as his customers had already started having it by rail.

Around the same time, there was another difficulty in arranging a delivery of coal to Sea Mills, when Thomas Sharpe sent a telegram asking Smart to send a vessel to load at Bullo at short notice. Not getting a satisfactory reply, Sharpe complained that it seemed very difficult to get any information and again asked Smart to say whether he could take the cargo from Bullo or not. Smart replied that the tides were not right to load coal at Bullo but Sharpe thought this was bosh and that the real reason for not going was because it did not suit Smart's purpose to load down. In spite of these hard words, the shipments from Bullo continued but not for long.

In July 1894, James Smart tried to reduce the price that coal factors L. Twining & Co. were asking for coal from Foxes Bridge Colliery to be shipped at Bullo. Smart claimed he had had a lower offer but Twining replied asking to see the quote in writing as he did not believe such a low price was credible. Soon after this, however, Smart's involvement in the carrying of coal to Sea Mills came to an end.

A likely factor in the ending of James Smart's coal trade between Bullo and Sea Mills was a heightening of concern about the hazard to navigation posed by the Severn Railway Bridge. Soon after the bridge was completed in 1879, it was found necessary to dump more stone around the major piers to combat erosion of the river bed and this exacerbated the eddies formed as the strong tidal currents rushed past the piers. These eddies could make steering difficult even in good weather and when the situation was compounded by adverse conditions, several experienced captains found themselves in trouble. Thus it was

Severn Bridge.

that as *Excelsior* was carrying coal down river from Bullo Pill on 4th June 1894, she collided with a pier of the bridge and Captain Watkins was knocked overboard by the tiller. Fortunately, he was picked up in an exhausted condition by some fishermen, landed at Sharpness and conveyed to Berkeley Hospital, where he recovered. *Excelsior* drifted on to the Lydney shore and was left there by the tide. Smart quickly arranged for *Flora* to go out into the river and lie alongside *Excelsior* so that most of the coal could be transshipped and after returning briefly to Sharpness, *Flora* set out again to deliver the coal to Sea Mills. The empty *Excelsior* was recovered, repairs were carried out and within two months the barge was back in service.

To make matters worse, while *Excelsior* was out of service, a more serious accident occurred on 5th July, when *Flora* also collided with the Severn Railway Bridge. While waiting to enter Sharpness with a cargo of Chepstow stone, the barge was carried past the entrance by the tide, and after the collision, she became a total wreck and the cargo was lost. Captain Henry Meadows and two men took to the boat and landed at Sharpness. Meadows had

The Severn Railway Bridge from the west bank. Note the wooden staging protecting the piers either side of the navigable channel. NP

Severn Trow Owners' Insurance Club letterhead 1894. MiP 2008.74/87

only taken over as captain a few weeks earlier, after previous captain George Everett had dropped out due to a cold and a chill. After these two incidents, it is not surprising that Smart gave up the Sea Mills contract.

Having no insurance on *Flora*, James Smart immediately wrote to his Member of Parliament (for Cirencester) about the dangers of the bridge and the letter was forwarded to the Board of Trade. He also got his solicitors to obtain a copy of the Act authorising the bridge but the outcomes from these actions are not known. Smart evidently learned from this experience, as he soon arranged insurance on *Excelsior* through the Severn Trow Owners Insurance Club. To replace *Flora*, in September 1894, Smart bought the barge *Wherry Packet*, which was about the same size but much older.

Less than a year after *Flora* sank, James Smart suffered another loss with the death of his long term captain Henry Watkins. As captain of *Flora* from 1879 to 1891 and then of *Excelsior*, Watkins had played a significant role in Smart's business, often making personal contact with customers such as William Jones of Chepstow and Thomas Sharpe of Sea Mills. In January 1895, he left Sharpness with a cargo of gravel for Bristol, accompanied by his step-son Thomas Dangerfield as mate. While there, Watkins suffered a thoracic aneurysm and died in Bristol General Hospital with his step-son beside him. A minor consequence of this was that a formal record of *Excelsior*'s movements in the second six months of 1894 was not registered with the Board of Trade by the deadline and Smart had to sign a formal declaration (with his cross) that the reason for this was that he thought the captain had done it but later found he had not.

In 1896, Smart sold the old barge *Wherry Packet* and replaced her with *Onward*, newly built by Matthew Gardiner at the Bourne yard near Brimscombe. *Onward* was similar to *Excelsior* with an open hold and a single mast, and she could carry up to 75 tons. However, like *Excelsior*,

she was too wide to reach Smart's wharf at Chalford and so did not go beyond Brimscombe. Smart arranged insurance through a national insurance company known as the Holman's Club. *Onward* joined *Excelsior* in the Chepstow stone trade and also made occasional voyages to Newport to collect manganese ore.

Official log of Excelsior, signed by James Smart with his mark after Captain Henry Watkins died on a trip to Bristol. GA D3080

SEVERN BRIDGE   S.W. VIEW.   W.P. 499.

A circa 1910 view showing the full extent of the Severn Railway Bridge from downstream. The navigable channel was through the right-hand of the two larger spans. NP

In the late 1890s, the main business for James Smart's barges continued to be carrying Chepstow stone to the Stroud Valley and wheat from Bristol, with occasional loads of coal, fertiliser and manganese ore from Newport, and timber from Bristol and Cardiff. Most barges left Sharpness empty, although there were several consignments of wooden boxes for the tinplate works at Lydney and occasional cargoes of gravel for Bristol. However, business declined due to competition from the railways, the wheat traffic from Bristol ending in 1897 and *Excelsior* was sold in 1899.

One more loss needs to be noted, as James Smart's old barge *Industry* became yet another casualty of the Severn Railway Bridge. On 2nd September 1898, when managed by Herbert Field of Saul, *Industry* hit a column of the bridge and broke up, and tragically, her pilot Samuel Bush was thrown into the water and drowned. When the bridge had originally been proposed, Smart was one of those who had travelled to London to object to its construction, believing it would be a detriment to navigation. Bush was one of six river workers who then spoke in favour of the scheme but three of those six subsequently lost their lives in vessels sunk at the bridge.

Chapter 8

Stroudwater Canal

The cargoes that James Smart's boats and barges collected from the Midlands, the Bristol Channel ports and places in between, were delivered to a wide range of businesses spread out along the Stroudwater and Thames & Severn canals. The details of individual vessel movements were recorded in the tonnage registers of each canal company and when combined with surviving letters to James Smart from the 1880s and 1890s, they give a real insight into working life on the two canals when they were still playing a major role in the economy of the Stroud Valley.

Regular consignments of coal from the Midlands, Bullo Pill, Lydney and South Wales were delivered to cloth mills, factories and coal merchants, as well as to Smart's own retail business at Chalford. Much road stone from Chepstow and Bristol was carried to many wharfs for the various local highway authorities and (after 1890) for the new County Council, who took responsibility for the main roads. Other cargoes, such as timber, grain, bricks, minerals, artificial manure, sticks, iron pipes, sand, furnace slag and rags, were delivered to particular businesses as and when required. The main outward cargoes comprised timber products from the numerous valley saw mills and there were some other local products but many vessels left the valley empty. For most cargoes, Smart was just a carrier, with either the supplier or the receiver of the goods paying a freight charge but in some cases he was acting as a merchant, carrying goods he had purchased from a supplier.

Over the years, it is likely that James Smart's boats and barges delivered to all of the recognised wharfs along the Stroud Valley, although he did little business at the western extremity of canal. Two letters show that when one of his barges brought a load of smith's coal up from Newport, he did sometimes drop off a few tons for Framilode coal merchant William Jackson or Saul blacksmith George Gabb. There were also occasional deliveries of coal and road stone to Bristol Road Wharf.

Framilode coal merchant Frank Cookley, who had a yard close to Moor Street Bridge in the early 20th century. HA

The toll clerk's house at Saul Junction, with his office adjoining on the right. MM

A typical towpath gate at Stonehouse. NP

Boats and barges joining the Stroudwater Canal from the north, south or west reported to the toll clerk at Saul Junction, who recorded what each vessel was carrying, where it was coming from and going to, and what was the toll payable. This same information was written on a ticket given to the captain. Normally, James Smart was allowed to make a single payment at the end of each month but at times he was so late in paying that the Company demanded cash on entry.

It seems that the weight of cargo recorded was determined as much by convention as by measurement. When in 1882 James Smart asked for the removal of a recent increase of two tons in the weight of each boat load of Staffordshire coal, the Stroudwater Committee instructed the clerk to charge for the same weight as was accepted by the Sharpness Canal Co. By the early 1890s, each load of Staffordshire coal was recorded as 30 tons even though the same cargo was charged as several tons more by the neighbouring Thames & Severn Canal. Also, wheat was recorded at ten sacks to a ton, although 100 sacks actually weighed 11 tons. However, this changed in 1895 after tonnage rates were regulated by Parliament and charges were based on actual weights. Smart tried to claim that the resulting increase in cost would reduce traffic on the canal but the Stroudwater Committee insisted that they were acting *'in strict accordance with the present law'*.

Coal from Bullo was not covered by the same convention and recorded loads were usually in excess of 30 tons, probably based on the ticket given to each captain at the time of loading. Occasionally, the weight was checked later when it was weighed out at its destination and then an adjustment to the toll could be required. In one surviving letter, toll clerk William Fredericks reported to James Smart: *'The weight of coal per your boat Alice should be 38 tons 11 cwt instead of 36 tons. Amount of tonnage 4s 9d making with 3s owing by William Gardner 7s 9d. Would be very obliged if you will kindly remit me same per return as my books must be made up* [in two days time]'.

Another difficulty arose in assessing the volume of timber in a cargo of tree trunks. After Smart's barge ***Perseverance*** had brought five loads of round timber from Newnham in 1890, Stroudwater manager W.J. Snape became suspicious that the declared measurements were not accurate. He therefore required Smart to provide a note from the customer saying what quantity was in each barge before any more trips took place and when ***Perseverance*** arrived without such a note, she was held at Stroud. When Snape did get the information he had asked for, it showed that the cargoes had indeed been larger than declared and Smart was charged accordingly.

When traveling along the Stroudwater Canal, Smart's boats and barges were usually towed by two donkeys or sometimes by a horse, and it was not long before they encountered one of the many towpath gates that were a feature of the canal. These were required because when the canal was new, no provision was made for fencing off the towpath from the adjoining fields, and gates were needed at each property boundary. As time passed, fencing was provided in places but many fields remained open to the canal and the crewman walking with the horse had to open and close each gate as the horse passed through.

Eastington Wharf circa 1906, with a group of children posed at one of the Stroudwater Canal's many towpath gates. NP

*Eastington Wharf viewed from Pike Bridge, with coal merchant Zaccheus Whiting, his employees and his boat **Nellie**. HB*

At Eastington, the resident coal merchant was Zaccheus Whiting, who had his own boat bringing coal from the Midlands but needed James Smart to help out from time to time. For one such delivery, Whiting was not shown the relevant paperwork and wanting to be sure he was getting his usual discount for bulk purchase, he wrote to Smart: '*I fully expected the colliery ticket with all particulars. The manager of the Cannock & Rugeley [Colliery] I know makes a difference to you and to me by [us] agreeing to take a quantity, but of course business is business – no one else need know about that. Kindly send all particulars so that I can enter it'.* In the winter of 1895, Smart's boats made five trips for Whiting in one month but that was unusual. Eastington was one of the delivery points for Smart's barge that occasionally brought multiple consignments of smith's coal from Newport but this could have been for the blacksmith at the canal maintenance depot nearby at Chippenham Platt.

As well as coal, Zaccheus Whiting also had pea sticks delivered by James Smart but one load caused him much trouble. Wanting an urgent delivery which did not arrive, Whiting was forced to buy elsewhere, as his customer's peas were spoiling on the ground. Eventually

Smart's barge did arrive with a ton of sticks but Whiting could only clear space in his yard for half of them and he sent the rest on to James Butt at Stroud. The main cargo that Smart's vessels delivered at Eastington was stone for roads in the Wheatenhurst district. Some of this came from Chepstow in large blocks which were broken up by the inmates of the Wheatenhurst Union Workhouse that overlooked the canal. Also, in May 1894, four boats brought up 135 tons of Cornish stone which had been delivered to Frampton Wharf by the trow *Neptune*.

Smart's vessels also delivered stone to Stonehouse Wharf for roads in the Wheatenhurst district and one surviving

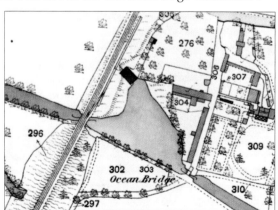

*The horse boat **Pioneer** being towed past the former railway-canal interchange warehouse beside the 'Ocean' at Stonehouse in 1911. GA GPS/609/13*
The 1884 1st edition OS extract (left) shows the siding on the embankment, with the warehouse built over a small dock.

Barge moored at Stonehouse Wharf, with railway wagons on the siding to the left. WA R1964

Extract from the 1884 1st edition 25 inch OS showing Stonehouse Wharf and its railway siding.

letter from stone merchant William Halling asked for the urgent delivery of 60 tons of broken stone and 300 [cubic] yards of cut stone from Chepstow. Other letters show that Smart occasionally delivered coal to coal merchant Charles Critchley and that he bought bricks from the Stonehouse Brick & Tile Co.

James Smart was occasionally asked to deliver coal to Ryeford when the usual suppliers were busy. Coal merchant Gilbert Hathway of the Haywardsfield Inn asked in one letter: *'Have you a boat up country you could let me have to load down?'*. In another letter, he wrote: *'Please send boat to Cannock & Rugeley* [Colliery] *for us. When do you think they will be there? Please tell them to load Old Side if they can. If you will let me know name of boat, I will send to colliery'*. Smart's boats also helped out coal merchants Wood & Rowe, based at Cheapside, Stroud but with an outpost at Ryeford. After one delivery to Ryeford, they wrote to Smart: *'You seem to have charged the full 30s Stroud tonnage on the cargo of coal you put out at Ryeford for us. Should not this have been charged 15s only?'*.

Smart's boats were very frequent visitors to Ryeford Saw Mills, bringing in huge amounts of round timber and taking away converted timber products and sawdust. The mill operators, Webb & Spring and for a time King & Scarborough, bought mature standing trees and arranged for them to be cut down and moved to a waterside location for collection by boats. Much timber was brought from Cirencester and Lechlade, and even from estates along the Thames Valley and the Kennet & Avon Canal. Most of this was converted into planks, staves and poles that were taken to the Midlands by boats which returned with coal. Some was made into boxes used for packing sheets of tinplate at the works at Lydney and sawdust was sent to firms that were curing bacon.

One surviving letter from King & Scarborough sought to co-ordinate the movements of their loading team with those of James Smart's boats: *'Our teams are hauling a quantity of timber into Dunsford Wharf* [Swindon] *which we shall be glad if you will bring up with as little delay as possible. We shall also be glad to see you with reference to our teams being at Lechlade Wharf when your boats are there'*. Another letter asked for a large barge to take 6,000 boxes to Lydney for the tinplate works and Smart arranged for ***Perseverance*** to take them two weeks

Ryeford Saw Mill workers gathered around the crane in their yard circa 1900. HB

later. As the mill did not have a means of weighing sawdust as it was being loaded, they regularly asked Smart to let them know the weight measured when it was discharged. King & Scarborough also had premises in the London area and one letter asked for the cost of taking round timber from Ryeford to Woolwich Arsenal.

Ebley Saw Mill in 1926, with many tree trunks waiting to be converted. VW

The boats were also very frequent visitors to Ebley Saw Mill, which was involved in the same activities as Ryeford Saw Mill and was managed by Webb & Spring in the 1880s and Thomas Mortimer in the 1890s. As at Ryeford, round timber was brought along the canal, mainly from the east but also collected from larger vessels at Saul Junction. The converted timber was mainly sent to the Midlands, although some went over the Cotswolds. In the 1880s, Smart's boats took nine loads of timber to London but sadly no details of these movements have survived. Some of the letters show that the mill also processed timber

Ebley Mill from the west, with another of the towpath gates in the foreground. NP

imported through Gloucester docks. At times, the mill generated so much business that James Smart could not keep up with it and one postcard complained: *'We have been expecting a boat to load goods for Birmingham. We have been obliged to send some by rail today'*.

An occasional cargo from Ebley was cider made by James Harper & Sons. In the 1890s, Smart's barges carried cider to Cardiff and a boat took some to Birmingham. Surviving letters show that Smart's boats also delivered bricks to Ebley for local builder Thomas Pitt.

James Smart's boats and barges carried a wide range of cargoes to and from Dudbridge Wharf, which served an important industrial area and was also a gateway to the Nailsworth Valley. Much stone was delivered for use on the local roads and coal was supplied to cloth

E.T. Ward's barge Ila at Dudbridge Wharf circa 1910, with the warehouse, crane and open yard behind. HB

manufacturers Apperly Curtis & Co. Grain was delivered to millers Kimmins, Drew & Co., corn merchant William Knight and brewers Carpenter & Co. The latter queried two of Smart's invoices, one because he had charged a higher freight than that paid by William Knight and the other because Smart had charged freight on a consignment for which the supplier was paying the charge. Bricks were loaded at Dudbridge for Chalford and Cirencester, much gravel was sent to Bristol, and local engineering companies sent three engines to Chepstow and one boiler to the Bourne. Also, a postcard from engineers Holborow & Co. asked Smart to send a barge urgently to High Orchard Wharf (Bakers Quay) at Gloucester, to collect a boiler that had been delivered there by the Midland Railway.

The wharf house and weighbridge (right) at Dudbridge. HB

Dudbridge Wharf as shown on the 1884 OS.

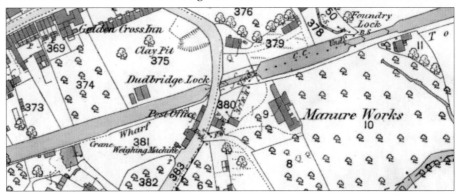

A view of Henry Workman's saw mills at Woodchester circa 1912. NP

Saw Mills, Woodchester, Glos.

Watercolour showing a boat unloading coal at Stroud Gas Works by Miss J. de M. West. MiP 1974.225/176. PP

Having ready access to the Nailsworth Valley, Dudbridge received cargoes of round timber destined for Henry Workman's saw mill at Woodchester. Smart's boats and barges brought loads from Cirencester, Chepstow and Newport. Further down the Nailsworth Valley at Inchbrook, the Boron Products Co. arranged in 1896 for Smart to start delivering to Dudbridge the raw materials they needed to make borax. In that year twelve boatloads (400 tons) of borate of lime were collected from larger vessels at Saul Junction and more arrived later. Meanwhile, over the next two years, Smart's boats made regular trips to Northwich in Cheshire to collect soda ash used in the production of borax.

James Smart's barges were occasionally asked to help with collecting coal from Newport for Stroud Gas Works, whilst they occasionally brought firebricks, fireclay and/or retorts from the Midlands or took away coke. Unfortunately, one boat carrying coke sank near the gas works in November 1896 and the Stroudwater Company had to lower the pound temporarily so the boat and its cargo could be recovered, for which the

Company charged Smart one pound. From the neighbouring sewage works, Smart's boats occasionally collected material *'suitable as manure'* and for nearby Lodgemore Mill, his barges occasionally brought coal for cloth manufacturers Strachan & Co.

From 1893, his boats and barges made many trips to Stratford Mill, Stroud, carrying wheat and some coal for millers Kemble & Dash, after Smart and the canal companies agreed to a competitive overall rate to secure the business. Stroudwater Company manager W.J. Snape wrote to Smart: 'I *will fix our rate at 8d* [per ton for wheat], *allowing 10 sacks to the ton, but if you charge for dead weight, we shall charge tonnage on the same'*. Kemble & Dash drew their wheat from Bristol, Avonmouth or Sharpness, depending on where they could get the best deal, and several surviving letters contain requests to collect particular consignments. Showing remarkable faith in the postal system and Smart's ability to respond, one card posted on a Friday reads: *'Bought this evening, a boat load of grain Sharpness to be moved tomorrow or Monday morning. Can you manage this?'*. Remarkably, the grain was indeed moved on the following day.

Stratford Mill itself was 400 yards from the canal, up the Painswick Stream which passed through a culvert under the canal, and the usual discharge procedure was to transfer the incoming cargo over the canal bank into punts which could be horse-hauled the short distance to the mill. After two years of operating in this way, Kemble & Dash wrote to James Smart saying they could not continue to take their grain by canal because their punts were badly out of repair and they were not disposed to spend money on them, especially as the railway company afforded them certain facilities. Faced with the potential loss of valuable business, the Stroudwater Company agreed to join Smart in contributing to the repair of the punts and the trade continued.

The main wharf at Stroud was Wallbridge Basin (also known as Wallbridge Lower Wharf) at the terminus of

CANAL SCENE, STROUD, LODGEMOOR BRIDGE.

Lodgemore Bridge, which provided access to Lodgemore Mill. HB

Advertisement for Wood & Rowe, coal, salt and builder's merchants of Stroud, 1902.

Wallbridge Basin painted by John Cook in 1931, showing the Company's warehouse and crane, with the chimney of Stroud Brewery in the background. NH

the Stroudwater Canal. Two locks above, on the Thames & Severn Canal, was Wallbridge Middle Wharf on the south side and Wallbridge Upper Wharf on the north. All of these were major destinations for James Smart's boats and barges bringing road stone, coal and a wide range of other cargoes. Much of the stone was delivered to the Stroud Highway Board for use on the local roads but some was transshipped from barge to narrowboat for delivery to other highway boards further east.

Much of the coal brought by James Smart's boats and barges to Stroud was delivered to local industrial firms, such as woollen cloth manufacturers Howard & Powell at Wallbridge Mill and Northcott, Cartwright & Co. at Woodlands [Peghouse] Mill. The latter were almost two miles from Wallbridge up the Slad Valley and one surviving letter asked Smart to call in to discuss hauling. As well as serving industrial firms, Smart delivered to local coal merchants such as Wood & Rowe and Miles & Jones, both using Stroud Upper Wharf. A surviving letter from the former also requested Smart to deliver some much needed bean sticks, whilst a letter from the latter asked for some smith's coal.

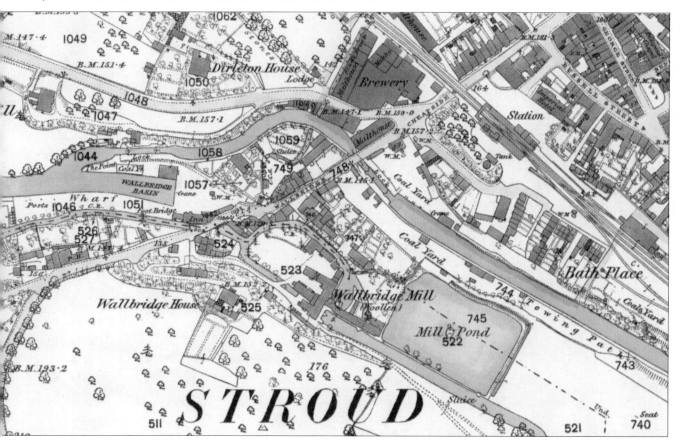

Surviving letters also shed light on some of James Smart's other customers in Stroud. Corn, hay & cake merchant William Townsend wanted to send one ton of moss litter to Kempsford, and to receive 23 tons of pressed hay from Frampton Wharf and 200 sacks of beans from Sharpness. Wood turners Ayers & Sons of Smalls Mill wanted to send staves to the Black Country and monumental masons Cratchley Bros asked Smart to call so they could settle his account. Animal feed manufacturer Richard Townsend wanted 300 sacks of beans brought from Sharpness and emphasised that he did not want them to be washed, adding: *'I prefer beans to water'*!

A key figure in James Smart's business life was W.J. Snape, manager of the Stroudwater Navigation Company, who was based in the Company's offices at the head of Wallbridge Basin. Snape was dedicated to promoting the canal in competition with the railways and he wrote many letters to Smart passing on offers of work and encouraging him to follow up new opportunities. In one letter, Snape reported that the Stroud Local Board of Health had for disposal free of charge a quantity of sewage manure suitable for agricultural purposes and he asked if Smart could deliver this to farmers around Chalford, Kempsford and Lechlade. Another letter reported that a Gloucester building contractor was due to build a house in Oxford and wanted to know the rates for carrying sawn timber, worked stone, slates, marble slabs and cement. Other letters reported that Spiller & Co. of Gloucester had 250 sacks of barley for the Cainscross Brewery, millers Kimmins, Drew & Co. of Dudbridge wanted 1,000 tons of wheat brought from Sharpness and a firm in Liverpool wanted to send 200 tons of flag stones to Gloucester.

Several letters to Smart show that Snape was particularly concerned about promoting canal traffic in competition with the railways. Having heard that the Stroud Highway Board were considering bringing stone from Clee Hill by rail in 1886, he persuaded them to try stone from Rowley Regis instead and he arranged for Smart to collect it. Noting that Brimscombe Gas Works was no longer supplied with coal by canal and that Allen Bros of Cirencester had sent 975 quarters of beans to Gloucester by rail, he asked Smart if he could find some way of winning back the

The Thames & Severn above Wallbridge Upper Lock in the 1880s, with the Canal Company's wharf and warehouse on the left. HB

traffic. When Snape heard that timber for Ebley Saw Mill from Gloucester was being sent by rail to Stonehouse and by cart from there, he asked Smart to let him have the railway rates so he could consider reducing the canal toll. Snape was particularly upset when he found that timber for new stables at Wallbridge Basin had been brought in by rail and he suggested Smart should call on the builder to try to get an order for other materials.

W.J. Snape also passed on to James Smart the occasional special job wanted by one of the mill owners on the Stroudwater Company's committee of management. One request from William Marling was to collect a boat load of blue bricks from Messrs Wood & Ivery's works at West Bromwich and deliver half of them to Marling's coal pen at Ryeford and the other half to Ebley Mill. In another request, Charles Henry Hooper wanted 6,000 fire bricks and some fireclay brought from Deepfields to Bonds Mill, and he agreed also to have about 2,000 blue bricks to fill the boat.

Snape also helped James Smart on operational matters, and Smart was sometimes able to return the favour. When *Perseverance* was stuck in the ice at Wallbridge, Snape let Smart know that the ice-boat was coming up the canal and would return the following day. He advised Smart to hasten the unloading to be ready to go down with the ice-boat, as it would be another two days before it went down again. When unable to attend a meeting with J.

Stroudwater Navigation Company clerk/manager W.J. Snape.

The headquarters of the Stroudwater Navigation Company at Wallbridge, which contained offices and living accommodation for clerk/manager W.J. Snape.

THE CANAL. EASTINGTON.

Dock Lock, Eastington, with the Canal Company's dry dock and canal maintenance yard behind. NP

Mills on the canal bank in the morning, Snape sent Smart the promised information and asked him to pass it on. When needing some practical work done at Ryeford, Snape wrote: '*Could you send as promised three good men with shovels to the Ryeford Railway Bridge at 6am on Monday next. Let them see Ted Hill at the Double Locks as they go down*'.

A more difficult matter involving W.J. Snape was the negotiation of drawbacks – temporary reductions in tonnage rates allowed by canal companies to encourage specific business. Having developed new traffic bringing stone from Rowley Regis and taking timber to Chippenham, James Smart declined to pay his tonnage in full in July 1887, claiming some drawback. Snape wrote explaining that any application for a drawback had to be made to the Committee and all tonnage had to be paid in full. When Smart refused to pay in full, Snape wrote that he had given instructions to stop Smart's boats moving unless they paid in cash. When Smart appealed, Snape replied: '*I cannot allow any drawbacks, having no authority to do so. I don't want to interfere with your trade, and the Committee would be pleased for you to attend a meeting and lay the particulars before them. If you go the proper way to work, you will find things will come right. Don't blame me for doing my duty*'. After this, Smart did pay his tonnage and he did attend the Committee in person but his application was refused. Three years later, however, he was given drawbacks on grain and timber taken to Chalford.

Chapter 9

Along to Chalford

As well as delivering to places along the Stroudwater Canal, James Smart's boats and barges also carried cargoes to wharfs along the Thames & Severn Canal. In November 1894, however, this traffic was interrupted by the collapse of the railway embankment alongside the Wallbridge pound approaching the viaduct near Capel's Mill. Following a period of heavy rain, a quantity of earth, stone and fractured retaining wall fell into the canal, and a large tree fell across the canal and towpath. The tree was quickly removed and dredging started but it took eleven days before Smart's fully laden boats could get through and a further twenty weeks before his fully laden barges could pass without lightening. Smart claimed £11 17s compensation for the delays to his vessels and this was eventually paid by the railway company.

The bridge leading to Capels Mill, with a barge discharging at the wharf just beyond and the GWR viaduct in the background. HB

Bowbridge Lock, with two donkeys waiting while a barge rises in the lock. MM

The first port of call along the Thames & Severn Canal was Capels Mill, where occasional cargoes of coal were delivered to the Stroudwater Dye Works run by W. Bishop & Son. It was common for customers to want prompt service and a typical letter from Bishop in 1886 asked for a cargo of lime coal *'as soon as possible'*. Smart also took coal to Gyde & Co's nearby dye works at Arundell's Mill.

At the next settlement around Bowbridge Bridge, James Smart delivered many cargoes of Forest coal, particularly for the use of the dye works managed by W.C. Chambers. One postcard from Chambers asked Smart to collect a cargo of coal he had ordered from the Park Iron Mines & Colliery Co. near Lydney. Unfortunately, the colliery was busy with other orders and there was a delay before Smart could pick up the coal from Sharpness. Not hearing anything for two weeks, Chambers wrote again asking when he could expect delivery, as he wanted the Forest coal to go with some Staffordshire coal that Smart had just delivered. In fact, by that time the Forest coal was already on its way up the canal and must have reached Bowbridge very soon after the letter was posted. For a subsequent order, the colliery initially wrote that the coal could not be ready until a week after the requested date as the mine was *'standing for improvements'*. A subsequent telegram said the coal could be ready two days earlier but by then it was too late for Smart to change his plans. In the early 1880s, Smart also supplied the saw mill at Bowbridge run by William Clark & Sons, bringing much timber from Cirencester and places in Wiltshire.

From 1889, James Smart's boats and barges carried many cargoes of manganese ore from Sharpness to Stafford Mill at Thrupp for paint manufacturers S.G. Bailey & Co. Initially, the ore came from Plymouth, where the Bailey family formerly had mining interests, but later imported ore came to Sharpness around the coast from Newport and Liverpool. Some of the ore was sent on by narrowboat to Stoke on Trent for use in colouring pottery. One surviving letter notified Smart that the schooner *Eva* was due to sail from Liverpool on Wednesday with 120 tons of ore and asked that barges be ready to meet her at Sharpness, on Saturday by latest to save demurrage.

A maintenance boat near Stanton's Bridge, with Stafford Mill in the background. HB

Smart's barges also delivered occasional cargoes of Newport coal to Stafford Mill but Bailey & Co. were inclined to be late in placing orders and they repeatedly ran short. In one surviving postcard, they wrote: '*If our barge is not likely to be up tomorrow, you had better send us a couple of loads of coal* [by road] *as we have only enough to last till tomorrow*'. They were no doubt relieved when *Flora* delivered 55 tons two days later. Soon after this, they again wrote: '*We shall be stopped for coal on Thursday next, so if barge is not likely to be up by Thursday, you had better let us have a bit to be going on with*'. This time *Flora* was on her way up the canal that very day but when they ran short again a few months later, Smart did not have a barge on the way and he had to arrange for an urgent delivery by rail and road.

Further along the canal, James Smart's boats and barges carried sticks, poles and canes to Griffins Mill for umbrella and stick manufacturer Charles Hooper. Many loads came from the Thames Valley via the Wilts & Berks Canal but one special consignment came from Lydney, comprising 15 tons of apple wood for making decoratively carved handles. One surviving letter delivered by hand asked Smart to collect a part load of sticks from Gloucester urgently and these were delivered two days later. Following a request to collect stuff from Thomas Adams & Sons of Gloucester, 25 tons of deals were delivered one week later and following a request to load at Pangbourne, 19 tons of poles reached Griffins Mill two weeks afterwards. After Charles Hooper died in 1893, the business was carried on by his sons. For a few years, they brought ships from the Baltic to Sharpness with 300 tons of birch poles at a time, each requiring Smart to arrange multi-vessel movements to bring the poles to Griffins Mill.

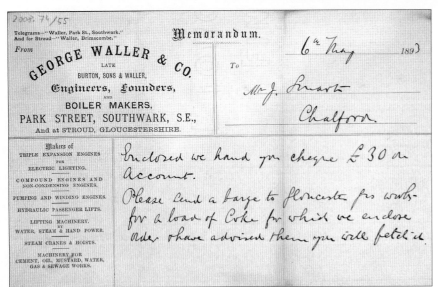

2008.74/55

Telegrams—"Waller, Park St., Southwark."
And for Stroud—"Waller, Brimscombe."

Memorandum.

From

GEORGE WALLER & CO.

LATE

BURTON, SONS & WALLER,

Engineers, Founders,

AND

BOILER MAKERS,

PARK STREET, SOUTHWARK, S.E.,

And at STROUD, GLOUCESTERSHIRE.

6th May 189

To

Mr J. Smart

Chalford.

Makers of
TRIPLE EXPANSION ENGINES
FOR
ELECTRIC LIGHTING.

COMPOUND ENGINES AND
NON-CONDENSING ENGINES.

PUMPING AND WINDING ENGINES.

HYDRAULIC PASSENGER LIFTS.

LIFTING MACHINERY,
BY
WATER, STEAM & HAND POWER.

STEAM CRANES & HOISTS.

MACHINERY FOR
CEMENT, OIL, MUSTARD, WATER,
GAS & SEWAGE WORKS.

Enclosed we hand you cheque £30 on Account.

Please lend a barge to Gloucester for works for a load of Coke for which we enclose Order & have advised them you will fetch it.

*A memo from George Waller & Co. asking for coke to be collected from Gloucester Gas Works in May 1893.
MiP 2008.74/55*

The wharf at Griffin's Mill was also used for loading bricks made on the Hooper family's land across the road from the mill and Smart's boats carried several loads to places over the Cotswolds. In one surviving letter, builder George Crook wrote: '*Will you kindly let me know what you can bring from 50 to 80,000 of bricks from Griffin's Mill to Cirencester wharf at per thousand, including carting the same from the field opposite Griffin's Mill to the boat*'. Crook was not happy with Smart's response but wanted him to take the job, and he wrote again,: '*The price you sent me is too high. If fine tomorrow morning, I may run down by the train due at Brimscombe 9.54. If you are anywhere near there at that time, would you see me there. If not, I may walk up to Chalford*'.

At the Phoenix Iron Works below Far Thrupp, George Waller & Co. made castings for their main engineering works in London and Smart's boats and barges delivered much foundry sand from Stourport, coke from Gloucester Gas Works and smith's coal from Newport. It seems that Waller & Co. were also not good at anticipating their needs and most of the surviving letters are about asking for urgent deliveries. In one letter they wrote: '*When will you now be able to deliver the load of red sand. We are quite out. Please send us two or three loads at once if possible*'.

When desperate for a delivery of coke, Waller & Co. sometimes also asked James Smart to deliver a small quantity by road from Stroud Gas Works to tide them over. In March 1893, they wrote: '*Please send a barge to Gloucester as soon as possible for some gas coke for ourselves, and kindly send in two tons from Stroud first thing tomorrow morning as we are quite stopped for it*'. Smart did not have a barge available but he did manage to send a boat load a week later. A few weeks afterwards, Waller & Co. asked for another delivery from Gloucester but it seems Smart did not reply and the firm sent five increasingly concerned postcards pressing for urgent delivery or at least news as to when the coke was expected. This culminated in a letter from Leo Waller saying: '*A barge of coke was ordered some weeks ago, and I regret to find you not only do not deliver but take no notice of our letter, causing us not only much inconvenience but considerable loss by depending on you. If you cannot execute the order or do not care to do it, better to say so at once, and we then know what to do. Reply by return will oblige*'. This ultimatum evidently worked, as *Perseverance* delivered 40 tons of coke four days later and a further 43 tons after another month.

Further along the canal, opposite Hope Mill, was the Canal Iron Works where Edwin Clark & Co. built steam-powered tugs, launches and passenger boats for the home and export markets. James Smart's boats supplied the business with foundry sand from Stourport and smith's coal from Newport. Surviving letters to Smart mainly asked for urgent deliveries, such as: '*Are you going to supply us with some foundry sand? We are quite out of it. If you can't supply us, we must buy some elsewhere*'. Also: '*When you are having some smiths coal up, please put us out 5 tons*'.

The next port of call along the canal was the large basin at Brimscombe, with the offices and

*Steamboat **Humaytha** built at the Canal Iron Works in 1905, when under the management of Abdela & Mitchell Ltd. MM*

warehouses of the Thames & Severn Canal Company. This had formerly been an important transshipment centre but now provided wharves serving local industries. The main cargoes carried by James Smart's boats and barges were road stone, coal and some foundry sand, while one unusual cargo was a pair of lock balance beams brought from Gloucester for the Thames & Severn Canal Co. After one delivery of coal, local merchant W.T. Buckingham wrote: '*I am very sorry to tell you that I can't promise you any money this week, but I will send*

Brimscombe Port circa 1906, with Canal Company buildings on the right. In front, beneath the covered roof, is the weighing machine used to weigh loaded barges. The Company kept a list of the boats that used the canal along with their dead weights, which could then be deducted to ascertain the load. NP

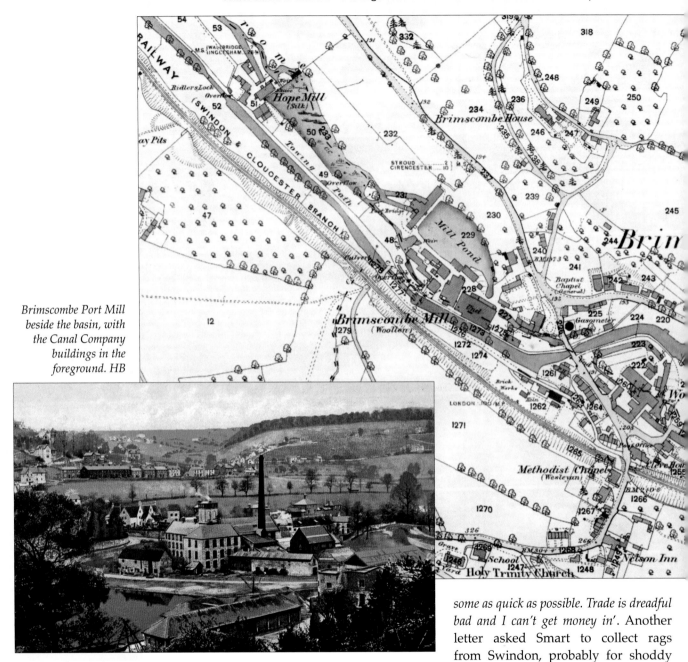

Brimscombe Port Mill beside the basin, with the Canal Company buildings in the foreground. HB

some as quick as possible. Trade is dreadful bad and I can't get money in'. Another letter asked Smart to collect rags from Swindon, probably for shoddy manufacturer Richard Grist at Lewiston Mill. Further letters show that Smart bought bricks from builder George Shaylor and was asked to carry away blocks of Painswick-type stone from Isaac Gardiner's yard, and to take sand from builders Wall & Hook's yard to Eastington.

James Smart's business was liable to be interrupted each winter by ice on the canal and if the cold spell lasted long enough, Brimscombe Basin provided a fine venue for skating. In January 1881, the *Stroud Journal* reported that a large number of adults and children were on the ice on Saturday and Sunday. As soon as there were signs of a thaw, however, an attempt was made to open a passage for boats by putting around eighteen men on the ice boat to rock it to and fro as it was dragged forward by three horses. In February 1895, the *Stroud News* reported that a carnival was held on the ice on Saturday which attracted many skaters and others, and some 2,000 people from Brimscombe and surrounding districts assembled to witness

The Thames & Severn Canal Company's warehouses and offices at Brimscombe. HB

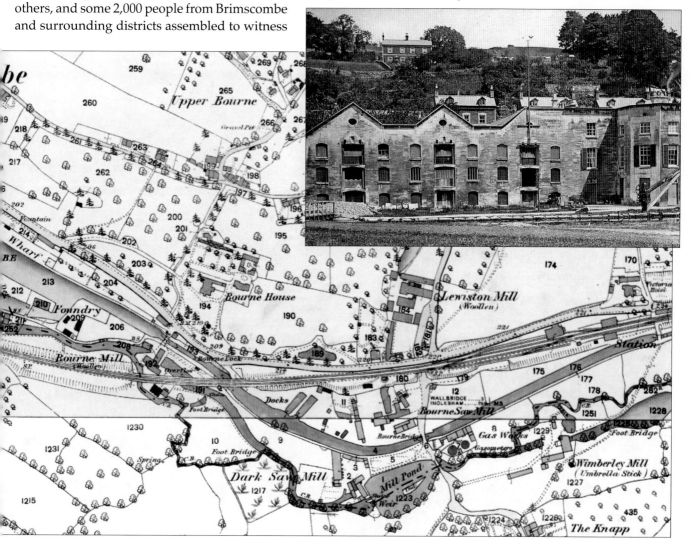

the scene. Lamps of all descriptions were hung around the basin, the Brimscombe Brass Band played lively music at intervals during the evening and refreshments were sold on the banks.

Just east of Brimscombe were three mills occasionally served by Smart's boats and barges. At Dark Mill, umbrella and stick manufacturers James Harrison & Co. ran out of coal one day and in desperation wrote to Smart: '*We shall not have a bit to start with in the morning. Please let us have some down tonight before half past five without fail*'. Bourne Saw Mill, run by Obed Philpotts, was one of several saw mills in the valley that purchased timber from as far away as the Thames Valley, knowing they could bring it home cheaply by water. At Wimberley Mill, pin manufacturers Critchley Brothers asked James Smart to quote for engine coal of the same quality as supplied to their neighbours Harrison & Co., giving separate prices for delivery to their yard or into their own carts.

Looking Down on the Bourne Saw Mill and Dark Mill circa 1906, with Brimscombe Gas Works behind and Wimberley Mill to the right. A train is approaching Brimscombe station; Smart occasionally had consignments delivered to the goods yard. NP

As Chalford was James Smart's home village, it is not surprising that it was a very common destination for his boats and barges. The main cargo was coal from Staffordshire or Bullo Pill, although the latter source declined in the 1890s when it became more usual for Forest of Dean coal to be carried by rail to Sharpness, where it was collected from the coal tip in the Old Arm. Coal for domestic consumption was delivered to Smart's own wharf for distribution around the area by road. Coal was also delivered direct to canal-side mills and factories, such as shoddy manufacturer W.C. Grist at Iles Mill and millers Clark Brothers at Chalford Mill. Once or twice a year, Smart sent a barge to Newport to collect a load of smith's coal, portions of which were delivered to blacksmiths and iron works along the Stroud Valley up to and including Chalford.

Smart's boats and barges also brought much road stone from Bristol and later from Chepstow, and the County Council established a special wharf alongside the road to the east of Chalford Chapel Lock. Grain arrived from Gloucester, Sharpness and Avonmouth, particularly for the Clark Brothers at Chalford Mill. Timber arrived from Gloucester,

*James Smart's boat **Flora** in Iles Mill Lock, Chalford circa 1905. HB*

James Smart's wharf at Chalford, with a boat alongside and his house to the right.
WA BW192/3/2/3/11/13

Sharpness and from over the Cotswolds, particularly for the Valley Saw Mill and the Victoria Joinery Works. Some bricks arrived from Dudbridge. Many small consignments of sticks were delivered to walking stick manufacturer William Dangerfied & Co. at his Bliss Mill complex, and occasional consignments of apple and pear wood may also have been destined for his works for making decoratively carved handles. Outward cargoes included staves to Birmingham, flour and bone dust to Bristol, and window and door frames (from the joinery works) to Gloucester.

In 1889, Smart's fleet of vessels delivered birch planks to walking stick manufacturer W. Dangerfield & Co. at Chalford, in June of that year three boats running all the way to Liverpool to collect 65 tons. This was followed by two steamers from Liverpool bringing planks to Sharpness, the first off-loading 126 tons into two boats and a barge, and the second transferring 227 tons into four boats and two barges. However, canal manager W.J. Snape noticed that the Gloucester newspapers reported that the first steamer had arrived with 150 tons, 24 tons more than had been recorded on the tickets, so he asked the clerk at Saul Junction to investigate. Unfortunately, no explanation of the discrepancy has survived but it could have been due to the convention used for determining the chargeable weight of timber on a boat, as Smart later complained that he had been treated unfairly by being charged *'according to the strict tonnage'*. Smart's fleet was called on again in 1894, when they carried 233 tons of birch deals from a ship at Sharpness to Chalford.

Bliss Mills, Chalford, where James Smart's boats and barges delivered timber used for producing walking sticks.
GA JV 13.1GS, 1904

One cargo of woodwork sent from the Victoria Joinery Works to a building project in Swindon led to a dispute about alleged damage to the cargo en route. The owner of the joinery works claimed that if there had been any damage in transit, the cost should be deducted from Smart's charge for the carriage. Recognising that the damage could have

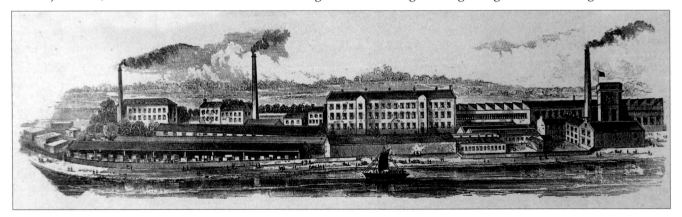

The Chalford Valley looking west circa 1895, with what may well be a Smart boat heading down past the skittle alley of the Red Lion pub with a load of logs for one of the saw mills. To the left is the site which was shortly to be occupied by Chalford station, opened in August 1897. HB

The Chalford Valley looking east circa 1908, showing Clowes Bridge and Red Lion Lock, with Sevilles Mill behind. NP

occurred during discharge, the master builder, who was from Chalford and evidently knew Smart well, called at the house of the carpenter involved and spoke with his wife. She said her husband had been drinking most of the previous day and had come home abusive and violent. She showed evidence of her injuries and told the builder he was likely to get a share of the abuse if he managed to talk with her husband. In spite of this warning, the builder told Smart he would call again and report further. Unfortunately, no further information about this dispute has survived.

In 1887, the Stroud Water Company began building a new pumping station beside the canal to the east of Chalford, to supply the parishes around Stroud with mains water, and James Smart obtained the contract for collecting the distribution pipes that were being manufactured in the Midlands. To meet tight delivery dates, as well as using his own boats, he arranged for other local boatmen to share some of the work. Word of this evidently spread, as Smart received a postcard from William Millard offering to bring a load down. Another postcard from Gloucester boatman William Green reported that he had arrived at Dudbridge with a boat full of pipes and he wanted Smart to provide men to get them out. Over a period of one month, twelve boats brought 420 tons of pipes to places between Dudbridge and Bowbridge. As this was new traffic that Smart had arranged, he asked the Stroudwater Company for a drawback on the standard tolls. The Committee agreed his claim would be considered when his contract with the water company was completed but the outcome was not recorded.

Valley Lock to the east of Chalford, with Chalford water works just visible in the trees.
GA GPS/609/22

Chapter 10

Over the Cotswolds

A s well as trading via Saul Junction in the west, James Smart's narrow canal boats also travelled eastwards over the Cotswolds into the Thames Valley and Wiltshire, with some going as far as London. The outward voyages carried road stone, imported timber and sawdust, and in return came English timber to be processed by the saw mills in the Stroud Valley. Smart's barges did not normally go east of Chalford, due to the poor state of the upper reaches of the Thames & Severn Canal and the River Thames. One Stroudwater Canal tonnage book does include entries indicating that Smart's barges took road stone to Siddington but the corresponding Thames & Severn Canal book makes it clear that the cargoes were actually transshipped at Stroud and taken on by narrowboat to any places beyond Chalford.

To the east of Chalford, the canal climbed the steep face of the Cotswolds to a summit at

Bakers Mill Lower Lock, east of Chalford, on the long climb up through the 'Golden Valley'.
GA GPS/609/22

Daneway Wharf with the chimney of the nearby saw mill behind the wharfinger's house and tree trunks on the wharf.
HB

Daneway and boatmen had to work twelve locks in two miles, with the intervening pounds narrowed by weed growth. In 1887, a holidaymaker in a pair-oar skiff noted: '*After you leave the last mills behind, you emerge on the back of Lord Bathurst's park at Oakley, and from this point to the end at Lechlade, the canal has at least the beauty of decay. So startling is this beauty that it is by no means unusual to find the channel narrowed to a space of ten feet between the weeds which cover the mud banks, even where they don't spread all over the space between*'.

Smart's boats regularly carried coal and road stone to Daneway at the top of the locks, including occasional part loads of smith's coal, whilst they took away staves and timber to Birmingham. Apart from the road stone, this traffic was connected with the saw mill and coal merchant's business run by the Gardiner family. The family also had their own canal boat and following the death of Job Gardiner in 1892, James Smart went out of his way to help his family keep the business going. When the Gardiners ran short of coal, they wrote asking Smart to drop some off as quickly as possible, and other loads followed to supplement those brought by their own boat. When they found a drum of oil was laying at Stroud station, they arranged for the Midland Railway Company to deliver it to Chalford by wagon and they asked Smart to send it on by boat or hold it until their own boat was passing. When they needed to replace their regular boatman, Smart offered them the services of his brother Jesse when required and also to see to the boat being done up in the Bourne dry dock. During the refurbished boat's first outing carrying staves to Birmingham, Jesse received a caution from the Local Health Inspector and he had to have the boat checked again by the Stroud Inspector.

The Daneway Inn was popular with boatmen who had worked up the long flight of locks in the Golden Valley but the moorings there were exposed to a south-west wind. One night, the wind was so strong that one of Smart's boats loaded with road stone broke free. It nearly collided with another of his boats loaded with sawdust but sank in mid channel before any contact. A few days later, a salvage crew with suitable gear was able to raise the sunken vessel and recover much of the cargo.

Just beyond the Daneway Inn was the entrance to Sapperton Tunnel, which was over two miles long. To avoid vessels meeting in the tunnel, entry was restricted to fixed times, with the permitted direction changing every four hours. Boats could be propelled by two men lying on a plank across the bow and walking along the sides of the tunnel but this required hiring a hobbler, as someone needed to walk with the horse or donkeys over the top of the tunnel. Alternatively, one man could push on a pole against the tunnel walls, although this was forbidden by the bye laws.

Canal Tunnel, Sapperton.

The Daneway portal of Sapperton Tunnel with the tunnel keeper's house adjoining. NP

Stone being loaded on to a boat at Trewsbury Quarry, to the east of Sapperton Tunnel, circa 1880.
CoM 1988/162/1

Along the summit to the east of the tunnel, the main destination for James Smart's boats was the engine house at Thames Head, worked by the Thames & Severn Canal Co. Coal was delivered to power the steam engine that pumped water from underground to try to maintain a good level in the canal. The freight charge due on this offset the cumulative tonnage charges Smart had to pay the Company. Nearby was a quarry known in canal records as Trewsbury (but also called Coatesfield), where Smart's boats occasionally loaded stone. Further east at Smerrill, timber was picked up and taken to Ebley in 1886.

At Siddington, beside the junction with the branch to Cirencester, Smart's boats delivered a few loads of road stone from Chepstow in 1891 and his boats occasionally carried Cotswold stone from Siddington Quarry to the Kempsford area. The quarry was owned by George Frazer and in 1891 he challenged Smart's account, complaining that he had been charged a higher rate than previously and for one load of someone else's stone. Eighteen months later, he quoted Smart prices for the supply of block stone and for thinner walling stone.

Beside the wharf at Siddington was a small maintenance depot and the office of William Pratt, who was responsible for the eastern section of the canal. This was one of the places that James Smart's boatmen asked for additional money to be sent to when they ran short. On one trip, Frank Gardiner asked Smart to send ten shillings to Pratt with the usual plea *'by return of post'* so his journey home would not be delayed. John Gleed asked Smart to send one pound '*as I must have a wheelbarrow*'. Another time, Frank Gardiner borrowed two shillings from Pratt on the promise that money from Smart was on its way but it did not arrive and Pratt had to write to Smart asking for repayment.

Siddington Junction, with the Cirencester Branch going away to the left, circa 1907. MM

The main cargoes carried by Smart's boats to Cirencester were sawdust, manure and road stone. After a few deliveries of sawdust from Ryeford Saw Mill in the 1880s, surviving letters show that a new phase of the traffic began in April 1893, following an inquiry from Cirencester bacon curers Cole & Lewis for sawdust to be delivered in bulk, not in sacks. The customer was evidently pleased, as further deliveries followed and local horse dealer Francis Townsend also asked for some shipments. As the sawdust was only weighed on discharge, the boat captain was expected to let the saw mill know how much had been carried in each boatload but reminder letters were sometimes needed.

In the 1890s, James Smart had contracts to supply road stone for the Cirencester District of the County Council. These required him to deliver a total quantity over a period of

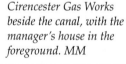

Cirencester Gas Works beside the canal, with the manager's house in the foreground. MM

time, allowing some flexibility in the timing of specific consignments. This usually meant deliveries could be fitted in with Smart's other business but occasionally the customer had unexpected requirements. One postcard from the District Surveyor asked Smart not to deliver any more stone for a while, as the County Surveyor had ordered 110 tons from rival carrier T.H. Pearce. As it happened, a cargo of stone was already on its way up the Stroudwater Canal and Smart had to arrange for it to be held at Wallbridge.

The main return cargo from Cirencester was round timber destined for saw mills at Ebley,

Ryeford and Woodchester. Some pieces were brought to the canal basin by timber dealer William Lock, who left them there to be collected by the next boat that called. In one letter, he asked Smart to send over a timber carriage to move a load of poplar and offered to provide overnight stabling for the horses. Another letter urged Smart to send boats to take away some oak before the usual summer drop in water level made boat movements difficult and another asked him to remove some elm which was preventing Lock bringing any more to the wharf. Some pieces of timber were so large that the local crane needed to be used, the charge for which could add 25 per cent to the canal toll. Rather than incur this charge, boatman John Gleed recruited help to roll the timber in. Another boatman reported he had been delayed while the timber he was due to collect was measured properly. At other times there was a shortage of timber and boats worked up the arm to the basin only to find there was nothing to collect, particularly if rival carrier T.H. Pearce's boats had got there first. Most letters from boatmen included a request for money to be sent to them at Cirencester or to William Pratt at Siddington for collection on the way home.

*Coal being unloaded from **Staunch** at Cirencester Basin in 1904.*
GA D2899

On one visit to Cirencester, two of Smart's boatmen were spotted fishing in the canal, which was against the Canal Company's bye laws. At the local Petty Sessions, James Davis was fined 2s 6d for fishing with a net and George Gleed was also fined 2s 6d for throwing stones to drive the fish into Davis's net. However, Smart appealed to the management of the Canal Company and they agreed not to press the charges on condition that the men promise in writing not to infringe the regulations again.

Coal merchant Frank Gegg beside the deserted basin at Cirencester circa 1920. GA D2899

James Smart often attended Cirencester's Monday Market to keep in touch with his contacts in the area and several surviving letters refer to matters to be discussed at such visits. N.W. North of Kempsford wrote that he wanted to talk about how coal and faggots could make an economic load. Jonathan Bowley of Kempsford wrote that he had deducted 2s 6d from Smart's account, because he had advanced that amount to a boatmen whose name he did not know but who he would describe when he next saw Smart in Cirencester. Edward Gardiner of Sapperton explained that he had not attended the last market as he had been at home harvesting but hoped to see Smart on Saturday at Gloucester Market. George Wicks of Cirencester said he had a six year old cart horse for sale that he would be pleased to show Smart the next time he came to Cirencester. George Frazer of Siddington Quarry wanted to talk about moving a load of stone by boat and Emanuel Curtis of Cricklade expected Smart would want to buy his pony when they met on Monday, as it was very quiet and good at work.

Smart's boats called only rarely at South Cerney, Cerney Wick, Latton and Eysey, bringing small loads of manure or imported grain or timber. The few return cargoes included gravel from Cerney Wick and some locally grown grain and timber. In one surviving letter, farmer R. Smith offered Smart a load out *'if you have a boat coming by.'* After one boat passing through Cerney Locks had lost a block overboard, a letter from lengthsman G. Millard assured Smart that he had recovered the block the same day it was let in and eight or nine days later he had put it on board Fred Meecham's boat for him to take back to Chalford. However, Latton was an important place for Smart's boats, as many turned south there on to the North Wilts Canal, heading for Swindon and the Wilts & Berks Canal. This was the usual means by which Smart's boats accessed the River Thames and it will be covered in

South Cerney Upper Lock. MM

The Locks, South Cerney

the next chapter. Normally, it was only boats trading to Marston Meysey, Kempsford and Lechlade that continued east along the Thames & Severn Canal.

James Smart's boats carried many cargoes of road stone to Marston Meysey in the early 1890s and he received several letters from the Gloucestershire County Highways District Office at Horcutt near Fairford about specific deliveries. At one time, so much stone was being delivered that the wharf became congested and District Surveyor William Yells asked Smart not to leave any more stone at Marston until the Kempsford deliveries were finished. He said that boatmen had thrown the stones all over the place and the road haulier had been very slack in moving them. As a result, there was great complaint locally as no one could get to the canal to load other boats. However, Yells added that if Smart wanted to send more stone soon, he would try to get what was there moved to make space.

A few months later, the excess road stone had evidently been cleared and Smart was asked to deliver 150 tons of stone to Marston Wharf, of which about 40 tons was needed urgently so the surveyor could finish a road he was in the process of rolling. Fortunately, Smart already had three boats on the way carrying 50 tons and, following a second letter, five more boats delivered the remainder a month later.

Smart's boats did not normally carry coal as far east as Marston Meysey and when two boats did make the trip in 1893 with coal from Bullo, their unloading was badly delayed. At Marston Mill, they had to wait three days for the horses to return from threshing duties at Fairford and at Marston Wharf they happened to arrive at the time when access was impeded by piles of road stone. Boatman William Gardiner reported to Smart that they would have a hard job to discharge the coal, as the stone was *'all rucked up'* along the water's edge from one end of the wharf to the other and some of it had fallen into the water. Then, thinking of his return journey, he asked Smart to let him know if any corn was sold at Cirencester Market that needed carrying away from Marston, suggesting that if Mr Bowley was at the market, he could bring back word. Four days later, Gardiner wrote that they had loaded 40 bags of barley for Brimscombe and some wheat for Cirencester, and he asked Smart to send ten shillings as they had run out of money. He

added that they had weighed out 22 tons of coal at each location and the customer had sent a man to check the amount at each place.

Lengthsman's round house beside the bridge at Marston Meysey. MM

Crooked Bridge (on the road between Marston Meysey and Castle Eaton) was not a common destination for James Smart's boats but seven loads of Siddington stone were delivered there in the summer of 1890. Crooked Bridge also featured in 1893, when Smart supplied bricks for the abutments of a wrought iron bridge over the Thames at Castle Eaton (a half mile to the south east). This was being built by Maidenhead contractor Henry Hill for the Swindon District Highway Board. In April, Smart sent some sample bricks to Castle

Bridge over the Thames at Castle Eaton built with bricks supplied by James Smart. OHC D230431a

Eaton and attended a site meeting with Henry Hill and his site manager Walter Locke. Hill ordered some pressed bricks made by Samuel Jefferies of Dudbridge and these were delivered to Crooked Bridge. Hill also asked Smart to provide a punt on loan and to return a small punt to the owners of the Wilts & Berks Canal at Swindon. During May, Smart was asked to provide more facing and common bricks, and some walling stone and road stone, and with the work nearing completion in June, the contractor moved the punt to Crooked Bridge for Smart to collect. However, when Smart submitted his account, the contractor objected to being charged four pounds for the conveyance of the punt to and from Castle Eaton as well as one

Thames & Severn Canal Company's old wharf house at Kempsford in 1969.
WA BW200/1/97/21

pound ten shillings for its hire. He thought the total cost asked for would nearly buy the punt and he insisted on a reduction of one pound.

Cargoes carried by Smart's boats to Kempsford included stone for the local roads and small quantities of grain, manure and bricks as part loads in boats that also called elsewhere. Three boats delivered Siddington stone in 1893, and one delivered a boiler and some sand in 1888. Outward cargoes included round timber to Griffins Mill and a little grain. A letter from Gloucester corn merchants Thomas Robinson & Co. asked for just 50 sacks of barley to be carried from Sharpness to Kempsford for Mr E.N. Edmonds of Whelford Mill and this consignment was put on a boat that was also carrying barley to Lechlade. A letter from Jonathan Bowley, builder, timber merchant and farmer, reported that he had put 80 sacks of wheat on a boat for Holtham of Gloucester but the boatman had refused to take about 60 more sacks to Cirencester for Allen Brothers. Bowley asked Smart to order the next boat to call for these and he also asked him to send a boat load of Forest rubbles and to pick up a few logs of timber at Clutterbuck's of Gloucester as soon as possible. Other letters from Bowley urged the transport of oak planks from Ryeford Saw Mill and the delivery of stone to Inglesham.

The main cargoes carried by Smart's boats to Lechlade were grain imported through Gloucester or Sharpness, road stone from Chepstow and chemical fertilizer from Newport. In return, locally grown grain was carried to the mills at Gloucester and some timber was taken to the saw mills at Ebley and Ryeford. Several surviving letters to Smart were sent by corn merchant Edward Tovey, who was sending and receiving small quantities of grain. Having bought 50 quarters of barley at Sharpness, ex-SS *Austria*, Tovey wrote: '*Be sure to take it in during the long days* [to avoid any charge for demurrage]'. When Tovey had 20 quarters of beans to go to Gloucester, he wrote: '*Please say when you will have a boat at Lechlade, as if you can't take them soon, my customer will most likely have them by rail*'. In a postcard, Tovey asked Smart to note that he had given ten shillings on account to the captain of the boat *Edith*. Other letters complain of irregularities in Smart's accounts. In one, Tovey pointed out that his portion of a cargo was 25 quarters of maize, not 50 as charged. In another, he noted that Smart had included a load of barley that had not yet arrived but had only listed 20 of the 25 quarters maize delivered in July and did not mention at all 25 quarters maize received with 100 quarters barley in August.

It was not usual for James Smart's boats to carry coal as far east as Lechlade but in the 1880s he did deliver a few loads of smith's coal from Newport in spite of stiff competition from the railways. In one letter to Smart, merchant Matthew Hicks wrote: '*I can do with as much as you can bring along the canal in one boat. Let it be of good quality and as cheap as you possibly can put it. I have been offered Smith's coal by rail very cheap*'. It appears that Smart could not respond to this request but he did send a load eight months later. One of Smart's boats did carry coal through Lechlade and on down the Thames to Radcot but this was exceptional.

Some of the cargoes delivered to Lechlade were destined for customers in the surrounding countryside. One letter asking for 50 quarters of barley to be brought from Sharpness was written by grocer E.J. Chamberlain & Son of Faringdon. Another consignment of 50 quarters of barley from Sharpness was requested by miller Henry Gallaway of Broadwell

Parkend Wharf on the River Thames at Lechlade circa 1895.
CoM 1979/75/1

but unfortunately the agent sent it to Kempsford and Smart was asked to bring it on to Lechlade. Several letters concerned the carriage of grain from Sharpness for millers Jacobs & Son of Burford. Boats were requested to deliver 50 quarters of wheat bought from Lucy & Co., 50 quarters maize bought from Robinson & Co. and 50 quarters barley from R. & H. Adams, which was part of a large cargo delivered to Sharpness by the steamer *Cadoxton* from Nicolaieff (now Nikolaev) in southern Ukraine.

For each outward trip, James Smart tried to organise a return cargo but sometimes arrangements did not work out and letters reporting a delay often included a request for instructions or money to be sent *'by return of post'*. Lechlade merchant Matthew Hicks reported that boatman Webb had found there was no timber ready to be collected and so he was going to return empty. Boatman William Tenty wrote that the wheat he was due to load at Lechlade had been sold to someone else, complaining that he had come a long way for nothing. He said he was going to Cirencester to load timber and he asked for ten shillings to be sent to Cirencester Post Office. Boatman Henry Stephens reported that he had part loaded a cargo of grain at Lechlade but then the wharfinger received a letter ordering the bags to be sent by rail instead. He asked Smart to send one pound to Mr Pratt at Siddington for him to collect on the way home.

Counterfoil of a ticket for a cargo of wheat carried from Kempsford and Lechlade to Wolverhampton in 1909. MiP 2014.58/20.

Occasionally, a boatman was asked to return home the long way round by first taking a cargo to the Midlands, or he could be asked to go down the Thames to load felled trees from an estate on the river bank. Boatman Thomas Gardiner wrote that he had not been able to load about 80 sacks of wheat for Walsall, because there were no hurdles available to put in the bottom of the boat to prevent the sacks getting wet from bilge water. Rather than wait for hurdles to be obtained, he asked Smart if he should go down the Thames with Alfred Whiting, who was due to load timber at Basildon. He also asked Smart to send three pounds for Alfred Whiting to Buckland Post Office (on the way to Basildon), as Smart had promised Whiting the money but had not in fact provided any. Such was Gardiner's confidence in the postal system that writing on a Saturday, he asked for a reply to be sent on Sunday night for him to receive at Lechlade Wharf on Monday morning. It so happened that this was the weekend of the 1891 Census and the records show 29-year old Thomas Gardiner as captain of the boat *Brothers* at Lechlade Wharf, with 58-year old Richard Pegler as crew, and 60-year old Alfred Whiting as captain of the boat *Gem*, with 65-year old Charles Butt as crew.

Chapter 11

Wiltshire, Oxfordshire and the Thames Valley

As well as serving places along the Thames & Severn Canal as far as Lechlade, many trips by James Smart's boats involved turning off at Latton, on the way to destinations in Wiltshire and along the Thames Valley. The North Wilts Canal ran south from Latton to Swindon. From there, the western section of the Wilts & Berks Canal headed past Calne and Chippenham to join the Kennet & Avon Canal at Semington, whilst the eastern section ran to the Thames at Abingdon.

Although Smart's boats usually travelled to the Thames Valley via the Wilts & Berks Canal to avoid difficulties in navigating the upper reaches of the river, when boatman Walter Pearce reached Latton in December 1885, he faced a difficult choice. Expecting a severe frost, he feared he would get stuck in ice on the narrow North Wilts Canal and as the Thames & Severn ice boat was due to set off for Lechlade with other boats, he decided to follow them. Even so it was difficult, as the ice was three inches thick on the Kempsford pound and each boat had to provide one man to help rock the ice boat from side to side to force a way through. Worse was to follow, however, as when they reached Oxford, they found that part of the central arch of Osney Bridge had collapsed and blocked the channel. Pearce wrote to James Smart, reporting that they were likely to be stuck there for at least two days and he thought they should return from London *'the other way'* (*i.e.* via the Midlands), as there was so much water in the river that it would be difficult coming back against the flow.

For those turning south at Latton, the first main destination was Swindon, where James Smart's boats delivered timber imported through Gloucester and loaded home grown logs destined for the various saw mills in the Stroud Valley. In one surviving letter, Mr F. Workman of the Canal Office at Swindon reported that there was much timber lying on the wharf, with more being hauled in, and he asked Smart to send a boat for it after a stoppage

Latton Basin with the lock leading to the North Wilts Canal beyond, circa 1895. MM

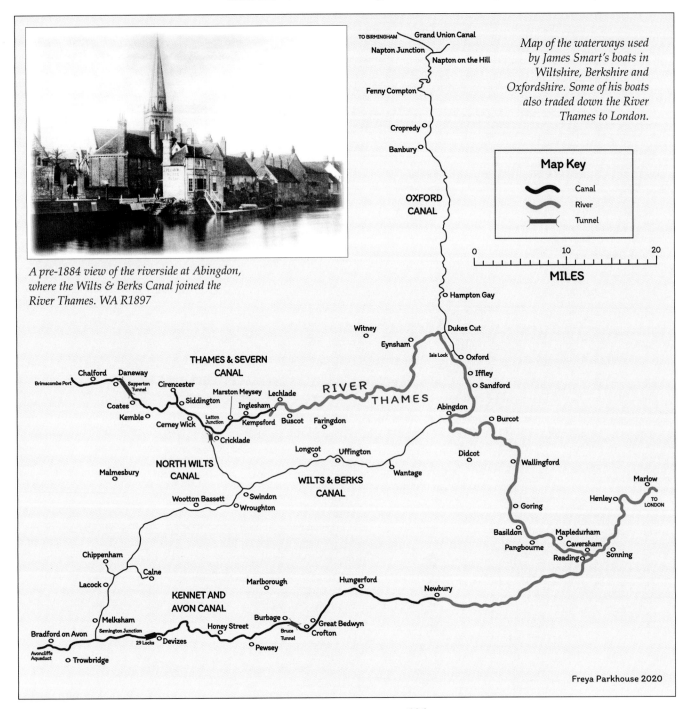

A pre-1884 view of the riverside at Abingdon, where the Wilts & Berks Canal joined the River Thames. WA R1897

Map of the waterways used by James Smart's boats in Wiltshire, Berkshire and Oxfordshire. Some of his boats also traded down the River Thames to London.

Map Key

	Canal
	River
	Tunnel

0   10   20

MILES

Freya Parkhouse 2020

planned for the following week. When loading timber at Swindon, it seems that boatmen sometimes needed to use a saw. In one letter to Smart, boatman James Davies wrote, '*We tried everywhere to get a saw to go to Swindon, but we could not get one, and it was no good to go there without a saw. John Gleed left his at home, so we thought it best to come here* [to Cirencester]'. Another letter from the Canal Office asked Smart to quote freight charges for delivering coal from Cannock and from Sharpness but there is no indication that this led to any business.

Having taken some deals from Gloucester to Swindon, boatman J. Webb was making enquiries for a return cargo when he heard there was a stoppage on the North Wilts Canal near Cricklade. Rather than remain idle for what could have been a week, he went home by train for a short break. When he returned to Swindon, he learned that the poles he had hoped to load would not be available after all and that the stoppage was still ongoing. He wrote to Smart saying that he had been offered a job collecting a cargo from Bristol but he really wanted to return home. While continuing to wait, Webb learned that a local miller wanted some wheat collecting but it turned out that the wheat had been sold to someone else. Then hearing that the stoppage would soon be ended, he wrote again to Smart saying he would make his way towards Cricklade. Meanwhile, boatman William Tenty had been stuck at Cricklade because of the stoppage and was desperate for supplies, as he had asked Smart for money to be sent but none had come. So he was delighted to receive some assistance when Webb joined him but he still wrote to Smart asking for 15 shillings to be sent to Cirencester, where he was expecting to load round timber once the stoppage was cleared.

Smart's boats passed through Swindon when on their way to Calne and Chippenham on the western section of the Wilts & Berks Canal. At Calne they delivered sawdust from the saw mills at Ebley and Ryeford for use at Harris & Co's bacon curing factory. At Chippenham they delivered boards from Gloucester that were used to make boxes for transporting tins of condensed milk made by the Anglo-Swiss Co. While on his way to Chippenham, boatman Thomas Gardiner was stopped in Swindon by the Local Board of Health inspector, who asked to see the boat's registration certificate. As Gardiner did not have it on board, he wrote to James Smart asking for the certificate, as the inspector was threatening to summons him if he could not show it when he returned through Swindon.

Boat at Chippenham Wharf on the Wilts & Berks Canal.
W&SHC P31603

To emphasise the urgency of the matter, he added: '*So you had better get me one as quick as you can and send him to the canal office, and if you don't send one I shall have to come and fetch one, so you know what to do*'.

The main return cargo from places all over Wiltshire was round timber, again destined for the many saw mills in the Stroud Valley. While loading at Wroughton Wharf, John Gleed wrote to Smart: '*When we have our load, there will be about another half load left to finish the lot. Would you please send 10 shillings to Cricklade post office*'. In the late 1880s, James Smart's boats even ventured to places along the Kennet & Avon Canal, particularly Dundas, Devizes and Burbage Wharf. While bringing home one load from Devizes in December 1885, boatman Thomas Gardiner was badly delayed by ice. In a letter to James Smart, he reported that he had had some difficulty getting along the Kennet & Avon Canal and after struggling further on the Wilts & Berks Canal, he was frozen in for three days near Lacock. The ice boat had run to Calne and he expected it would reach them the following day, allowing him to continue his journey home. He confirmed that he had also loaded five tons of sand, as Smart had ordered, adding: '*It was 18d per ton and I had to pay the wharfage on it*'. He asked Smart to send a postal order for 30 shillings '*by return of post*' for him to collect at Wotton Bassett Post Office.

Devizes Wharf on the Kennet & Avon Canal, circa 1900. WA D1674

Wantage Wharf, at the end of a short, three-quarters of a mile branch off the main line of the Wilts & Berks Canal, circa 1895. WA R2143

Smart's boats also occasionally traded to places along the Wilts & Berks Canal to the east of Swindon, including the carriage of timber to Longcot and Wantage. Some round timber was collected from the area as well. However, this trading was trivial in comparison with the many trips along this stretch of canal made by Smart's boats passing to and from the Thames to places such as Oxford, Reading and London. On one such trip, boatman J. Webb ended up buying a horse at Longcot that Smart's brother Jesse had reported was for sale. Webb reported to Smart: *'The owner let us try it on the boat down to Uffington, and I think it will do. He took the donkeys in exchange at 30 shillings, so I had to give £4 10s besides. As our donkeys was middling and one was very lame, I was glad to see the last of them'*. Due to this expenditure, he asked Smart to send £3 to Goring Post Office *'by return of post'*. On another outward journey, James Rossiter found himself short of money because he had not been able to collect the freight charge for a load of bricks he had delivered and he asked Smart to send one pound to the lockkeeper at Abingdon *'by return of post'*.

Throughout the 1880s, James Smart's boats carried many loads of imported deals from Gloucester to Oxford. For the return journey, these boats usually went north up the Oxford Canal, carrying a cargo if they could get one, and then they loaded coal in the Cannock area to take back to the Stroud Valley. In 1891, Gloucester timber merchants Thomas Adams & Sons Ltd asked Smart to carry loads to Banbury as well as to Oxford but a few days later they cancelled the boats for Banbury and the Oxford traffic also ceased. In the early 1890s,

Ridley's timber yard on the River Kennet in Reading, circa 1888. CMJ

Smart's boats carried imported deals from Gloucester to Reading and surviving postcards show that these were being sent by timber merchants Price, Walker & Co. Ltd and delivered to timber merchant George Lewis. Some of these boats went on to load Cannock coal but others loaded locally grown timber for the Stroud Valley.

Most of Smart's boats that delivered cargoes to places in the Cotswolds or further east returned home with round timber loaded at places along the Thames Valley, such as Pangbourne, Basildon and Goring. As some trees being cut were at a distance from the river bank, there could be difficulties co-ordinating with the sawyers. Thus it was when two boats captained by William Staddon and John Webb arrived at Pangbourne, they found there was nothing ready for them to load. William Staddon junior later remembered that while the two captains went up into the woods to see the saw men, the two mates decided to have 'tea for two'. Unfortunately, while crossing from one boat to the other, Staddon junior fell into the water and found himself trapped under the two hulls that were side-by-side. Desperately holding his breath and not knowing how to swim, he clawed his way along the bottoms of the boats until he popped up between the two sterns and then the other mate helped him out. When his father got back, he saw the wet clothes and remarked '*Oh, Willum's been in the water*' and he was never told how he had nearly lost his son forever.

To help James Smart co-ordinate with the sawyers, his returning boatmen provided what feedback they could but this was often too late to be effective. In one letter from Abingdon, Henry Crook wrote: '*We had a hard job for to get up the river. We met Stephens agoing down as we was agoing up, but I don't think as there is anything for him to put in. We shall try and get home as quick as we can if the frost don't stop us*'. Also from Abingdon, Thomas Gardiner wrote: '*James Rossiter began loading yesterday, and he is going to put a full load in at Basildon as there is about enough there to load him, and then there will not be any more there for a few weeks*'. Unfortunately, this information did not reach boatman W. Gardner, who arrived at Basildon four days later. He wrote to Smart: '*They cannot give me a full load, not for another fortnight. They have a little rubbish. I am going to take it in, and then go to Goring and take on the timber that is left there, which will make a load. Please to send me £1 10s to Goring post office by return of post*'.

Delays in loading timber became a particular issue in early 1893, when Charles Hooper of Griffins Mill was wanting supplies from saw mill manager William Flowers of Pangbourne, and the difficulties are recorded in a remarkable series of surviving letters to James Smart. While on his way to deliver deals to Reading, boatman Walter Pearce called in to see Flowers but he was not at home. He wrote,: '*I shall see him tomorrow morning. I think he has got plenty*

The Thames, Goring Lock

A barge loaded with logs approaches Goring Lock on the River Thames circa 1905, heading north towards Abingdon. DP

*Caversham Bridge on the River Thames at Reading, looking west circa 1890, with the narrowboat **Maggie** moored to the bank alongside a timber yard where she is probably discharging deals. DP*

of stuff ready but no one to haul it to the water. His wife told me he would have to let the saws stop to haul us in a freight. I cannot get anything to do here to suit us'. Ten days later, boatman Thomas Gardiner managed to meet Flowers on the way to Reading but did not get any firm news. He reported to Smart: 'Mr Flowers said he did not know whether he should be able to get anyone to haul the stuff or not. He said I was to call and see him when I came back up from Reading. Write to Reading post office and let me know if you have seen Mr Hooper or not, and let me know if I had better come on home empty or not if I can't get a load at Pangbourne. Also let me know if there is any poles at Wroughton Wharf or not, and when I get to Pangbourne I will write and let you know if I am going to load there as soon as I know'. When Gardiner returned

Postcard from umbrella stick manufacturer Charles Hooper asking for a boat to collect timber from Pangbourne in April 1893. GA D4848 SHEET 34

> From CHARLES HOOPER,
> GRIFFINS MILLS,
> Stroud, *April 11th* 1893
>
> Dear Sir, I have a boat load to send from Pangbourne. *[illegible]*
>
> Yours Truly,
> Chas Hooper

to Pangbourne, the situation was still unclear. After waiting two days, he wrote to Smartt: '*I have seen Mr Flowers last Friday morning, and I have been waiting here to know if he could get a load hauled in.* [Now] *he has seen the man that is going to haul it in, and he cannot haul any in until after Easter*'.

A month later, two boats visited Pangbourne, this time by prior arrangement, but there was still a delay. Boatman Walter Pearce wrote to Smart: '*We wrote to Flowers on Saturday to tell him we should be here to start loading on Tuesday morning, but*

Horse-drawn boats on the River Thames near Shooters Hill, Pangbourne. WA R1923

he did not come and we had to go over in the woods to him to see what he had to say. There is a lot more heading than one boat will take and a part of a load of staves and squares, and there is a lot of heading to come from the saws. [But] *he has got the traction engine at work, hauling to the station sticks and slabs, and he would not stop him from hauling to start on us till he has finished. We expect to have some of it hauled in tomorrow. We will write and let you know when we are loaded*'. Six days later, he wrote again: '*We shall finish loading tonight or the first thing in the morning. Please send us twelve pounds by return of post to Abingdon post office. We have got a boat load and a half of heading and the remainder staves and beech squares. Be sure to send to Abingdon by return not to keep us waiting*'.

It seems that the boatmen accepted that some delays in loading and unloading were a part of the job but they were paid for the trip and not by the hour, and it is clear they really did not like having to hang around waiting for their money to arrive. Virtually every request to Smart was accompanied by the plea to respond '*by return of post*' and it seems that he usually did so and the post was remarkably reliable. However, after one request from William Tenty at Pangbourne was not answered in two days, he wrote again saying: '*I have not had any money or letter from you, and I put the address all right. I have been to Goring post office that is six miles from Pangbourne. I cleared all from Basildon and finished loading, so I am waiting for a letter from you*'. Another request for money followed an unexpected encounter while boatman Frank Pearce was returning from a trip down the Thames. He wrote to Smart: '*When I was at Wallingford, a man had a donkey for sale and he wanted three pounds for him. So I made a chap with same, so I have not got any money now. Please to send me one pound ten shillings by return of post to Wantage as I shall get there on Thursday morning*'.

Although most of the timber collected by James Smart's boats along the banks of the Thames was carried back to the Stroud Valley, some was taken up the Oxford Canal to the Midlands. On one such trip in February 1884, two boats were held up at Oxford because the canal bank had

The steep sided cutting on the Oxford Canal near Fenny Compton, that was left after opening a former tunnel. The aqueduct was required to carry a former watercourse. WA BW192/3/2/2/19/9

slipped badly at Fenny Compton, where a former tunnel had been opened to form a steep sided cutting. As it was likely to be a long stoppage, the two captains, John Webb and William Staddon, went home by train, leaving the boats in the care of a boatman and 13-year old William Staddon junior. Once the slip was cleared, the two captains were summoned back by telegram, only to be greeted by the news that the other side of the cutting had also slipped. With the prospect of another long stoppage and no money for another train journey, all four set off at 7.00am to walk back to Chalford. William junior later recounted how he started the walk excitedly, running to and fro across the road, but by the time he was nearing Bisley, he was crying and his feet were bleeding. His father suggested he could stop off at the police station until he felt better but this did not appeal. So he kept going, hardly able to shuffle along, eventually arriving home almost 24 hours after setting off. When the stoppage was eventually cleared, the crews returned to their boats and finished their journey to Birmingham. From there, they went on to the Cannock area to load coal before returning to Stroud six weeks after the initial hold up.

*The horse-boat **Three Sisters** heads north through Napton Locks at the top end of the Oxford Canal, near its junction with the Grand Union Canal for Birmingham and the Midlands. NP*

A trip up the Oxford Canal in the following year involved two boats in the charge of John Webb and Walter Pearce. After both had taken road stone to Cirencester, they went down the Thames to load timber at Pangbourne and then Webb sent a letter to Smart from Wallingford reporting that loading had been delayed, as 'Old Flowers' was a fortnight behind his time. The staves were mostly long lengths and 'as green as grass' and Pearce had been obliged to take some of them 'on top of the timber'. Webb asked Smart to send more money to Banbury, as much of their load was for Willenhall and Wolverhampton, for which there would be more tonnage to pay than for Birmingham. He also asked Smart to report the extra tonnage to Mr Hooper, for whom the cargo was being carried, and to seek additional payment. A few days later, Webb wrote from Cropredy to say they were having to go very steadily up the Oxford Canal as they had such big loads on and he did not know how they would have managed if the recent rain had not filled the cut. He asked Smart to send orders for collection at the Bar Lock at Birmingham, saying where they were to load coal to bring home. Both boats eventually returned to Chalford just over a month after leaving.

During another trip up the Oxford Canal, Thomas Gardiner wrote from Banbury again asking what coal Smart wanted brought back to the Stroud Valley, in this case requesting the orders be sent care of the Warwick & Birmingham Canal Office at Camp Hill, Birmingham. Gardiner also reported that his young crewman had left him and he asked Smart to send Richard Pegler as a replacement if available. Such was his confidence in the postal system and in the speed of Smart's response that he suggested Pegler should meet the boat at the bottom of the Hatton flight of locks (near Warwick), where he expected to be the following evening.

The Cannock Extension Canal at Hednesford was one of the places where James Smart's boats headed to load coal before returning home from a long trip. JR

Horse boats at Banbury. WA BW197/4/1/1/89

Most years, one or more of James Smart's boats travelled all the way to London carrying timber from Ebley Saw Mill (and sometimes also from Ryeford). Usually, the boats travelled on to the Midlands, presumably carrying whatever load they could obtain, and then collected coal to bring back to the Stroud Valley. A few boats made this triangular journey in the opposite direction to collect goods from London, including two bringing sticks to Griffins Mill in 1886 and two with special cargoes of wool for Bonds Mill in 1890. A curious letter from London enclosed a cheque in payment for coal for St. Pancras Workhouse, with a complaint about a great delay in delivering a sample of tiles – presumably the coal had been carried from the Midlands and there had not been a later opportunity to deliver the tiles. These round trips could be done in four to five weeks but some boats were away for two months or more.

In August 1893, Jesse Smart took a cargo to London that he had picked up on the way after delivering grain to Lechlade. His arrival was reported in a letter from W.E. Wells of Belvedere Road, Lambeth, saying that Jesse had been promised a return load of deals for Reading and he wanted a postal order for £5 to be sent by return of post. It seems that the writer was a partner in the firm of Martin, Wells & Co., builders, of Acre Wharf at the Westminster Bridge end of Belvedere Road.

Westminster Bridge as viewed from Lambeth Bridge on 30th July 1897. Acre Wharf can just be glimpsed through the end span on the right. NP

Chapter 12

Trouble over the Summit

The route over the Cotswolds involved traversing the lengthy summit level of the Thames & Severn Canal, including the $2^1/_4$ mile long Sapperton Tunnel. The tunnel had been cut through limestone and needed a clay lining to retain water. However, it proved difficult to keep this lining in good condition and in the summer months there was often more leakage than could be made up by the nearby steam pumping engine. If the summit level dropped too much, it became necessary to transfer some of a boat's cargo to another boat and in extreme cases, boats could not pass at all. Several surviving letters to James Smart show that his boatmen did their best to mitigate any difficulties by seeking advice in advance. When three boatmen returning from the Thames Valley were concerned about whether they would be able to get over the summit, they asked Smart to write to the canal office at Siddington to ask whether they would need an extra boat to take some of their cargo over the top. In a similar letter from Abingdon, Thomas Gardiner wrote: '*Please send a postcard to Swindon canal office and let us know how much water there is in the summit. We are drawing about two feet seven* [inches]. *Let us know if you are going to send anyone to lighten us down home*'.

The Daneway portal of Sapperton Tunnel on the summit level of the Thames & Severn Canal, circa 1900. MM

The level of water in the summit became even more of an issue in the summer of 1886, when traffic was stopped for a time and James Smart became embroiled in company politics. By this time, the Thames & Severn Canal had come under the control of the Great Western Railway Company and they had stopped the pumping engine on the grounds that it was not cost effective. Knowing that the water level would be low, Smart arranged for a boat loaded with 20 tons of sawdust at Ebley Saw Mill to transfer half of its cargo to another boat at Brimscombe and the two made their way to the summit. Finding that the water level was lower than expected, the first boat off-loaded half of its depleted cargo and just managed to get through the tunnel, with only 5 of its original 20 tons of sawdust. The second boat was not so fortunate, as it became stuck in the locks on the way to the summit. On the following day, another of Smart's boats was returning from London with 24 tons of special timber for walking stick manufacturer Charles Hooper and although this was shared with two other boats, all three became stuck at the eastern end of the tunnel, where more boats were also waiting.

A few days later, James Smart attended a meeting in Gloucester with W.B. Clegram, engineer of the Sharpness Dock Company, who was co-ordinating a group of canal companies that wanted to take control of the Thames & Severn Canal to keep it operating effectively. Smart's evidence was then used in a letter to the Board of Trade blaming the difficulties on the Great Western Railway Company management and seeking legislation to authorise transfer of ownership. This was followed up by a memorial to the Board of Trade, which was signed by a large number of land and mill owners, barge and boat owners, and traders on the canal. By this time, however, boats were moving again and nothing was done.

Three of the locks on the climb up to the summit level at Daneway, with the embankment of a side-pond in the foreground.
WA R1974

While all this was going on, and not knowing how long the difficulties would take to resolve, James Smart tried a different way of supplying walking stick manufacturer Charles Hooper, whose goods were stuck the wrong side of the tunnel. As noted in an earlier chapter, in September 1886 Smart sent his barge *Industry* to Bristol and along the Kennet & Avon Canal to reach the Thames Valley, and it returned with 45 tons of sticks. While this effort was no doubt appreciated, it was not repeated and trade to and from the Thames Valley had to accept the vagaries of the water level on the summit.

The Locks, near Sapperton.

A view in the opposite direction, looking down the triple Siccaridge Wood Locks flight from Daneway circa 1905. NP

Low water in the summit caused difficulties again in July 1887, when two of Smart's boats with light cargoes were stuck on their way up the locks, the scene being observed by a holidaymaker sculling a pair-oared skiff. As the sculler came in sight of the summit, he saw seven locks ahead of him with narrowboats stuck in five of them. Rather than wait until it rained, he persuaded the boatmen to lift his skiff out of the water, use two donkeys to tow it up the towpath and then put it back in at the summit. It seems that light cargoes in the summer and the occasional hold up thereafter became the norm, at least for a few more years.

In the early 1890s, James Smart's boats were doing good business carrying to and from places in the Thames Valley and Wiltshire but movements were very dependent on the water level in the summit of the canal and the issue came to a head in 1893. Smart did his best to manage the difficulty by sending only light loads over the summit during the summer months but he must have been worried when he received a letter from boatman William Tenty reporting difficulties in getting to Cirencester as early in the season as the beginning of May. Although only carrying 13 tons of sawdust, Tenty reported that he had had to lighten his cargo to get up the arm and then go back to collect what he had off-loaded. Another load of sawdust at the end of June got stuck on the way to the summit and this led Messrs King & Scarborough at Ryeford Saw Mills to write to Smart: '*Mr F J Townsend informs us that the boat load of sawdust which left here on 26 ult for him has not yet arrived. Has this gone to*

Coates round house and nearby railway bridge, with the summit level under restoration in 1904. WA R1992

the bacon factory [at Calne] *by mistake? Kindly say at once'*. Few other boats crossed the summit that summer and those that did carried very reduced loads.

Shortage of water was also a problem on the Wilts & Berks and the North Wilts canals that summer. When returning from the Thames at the end of August with a cargo of sticks for Griffins Mill, John Gleed had to off-load part of his cargo twice. From Swindon he wrote to James Smart: *'We had to lighten at Abingdon. We fetched a lighter from Wantage and had got it all to Swindon and have taken the lighter back. We have had to put out five or six tons at Swindon Wharf. Please to send to Mr Pratt to let me know where the punt is so we can have it to fetch our lightning'*. It seems they did not go back to collect their 'lightening', as six weeks later the manager at Swindon Wharf wrote to Smart: *'The sticks your boat put on our wharf are still there and spoiling: shall we warehouse them at your expense, or can you send for them?'*.

The regular seasonal problem of low water on the summit due to leakage was made worse in 1893 because the pumping engine at Thames Head was only worked intermittently and with a dry autumn, the depth of water on the summit was only two feet at best and sometimes not even one foot. To avoid the difficulty, James Smart set about arranging for one urgent load of timber from the Thames to be brought back via the Midlands. He contacted the Birmingham office of the Worcester & Birmingham Canal and William Hodgkins replied: '*Mr George will let the converted timber pass from the Stratford Canal to Worcester at 10d per ton. The rates on the other canals will be about as follows: Oxford Canal 1s 4d per ton, Warwick Canal 9³/₄d per ton, Stratford Canal 7d per ton, making a total together of 3s 6³/₄d Oxford to Worcester. If it will be any advantage to you, we will give you declarations to clear you through on the various canals and you can send us a cheque for the tonnage altogether*'. Smart evidently accepted this offer, as the declarations were sent and the boat reached Griffins Mill only two weeks after the original letter.

Other regular customers were not so fortunate and Smart received several letters expressing concern about delayed cargoes. Edward Tovey of Lechlade wrote: '*Please let me know when I shall receive the 50 quarters barley put in your boat some weeks since*'. Jacobs & Son of Burford wrote: '*Messrs J. Reynolds & Co.* [Gloucester] *say they have not heard of the 35 quarters of wheat. Please explain, as we are advised that it was delivered to your boat at Lechlade Wharf on the 19th inst* [six days ago]'. Kemble & Dash of Stratford Mills were particularly scathing and demanded a reduced freight charge, writing: '*We shall be glad to know what you will allow us on the 200 sacks wheat just delivered us from Lechlade. Eight weeks in transit is not to be endured, and as this is not by any means the first time we have had to complain of delay, we must insist now on you calling and making some arrangement with us. We cannot think of ordering any more grain by water from the districts above us on the canal*'.

While James Smart was busy doing his best to cope during this difficult time, he also tried

The pumping engine house at Thames Head. WA R1989

to get something done about the declining condition of the Thames & Severn Canal. To this end, he worked with Stroudwater Canal manager W.J. Snape to prepare a memorial to local Members of Parliament detailing the poor state of the canal and urging them to bring the matter before the proper authorities. Between them, they collected 151 signatures from local manufacturers, traders, barge and boat owners, and anyone interested in the continued operation of the canal, including a dozen of Smart's boatmen.

To back up the memorial, Snape and Smart also collected letters from traders highlighting specific difficulties due to low water levels in the summit pound. King & Scarborough of Ryeford Saw Mills wrote that they had been very greatly inconvenienced by not receiving timber from Lechlade, Swindon and Cirencester, and they had known timber to lay on wharfs for months before they could get it home. Henry Workman of Woodchester Saw Mills wrote that he had purchased timber in close proximity to the canal, relying on being able to convey it by water (the nearest railway stations being many miles away) and yet it had remained on the wharfs for months because the boats could not get through. Samuel Jefferies of Dudbridge and Stonehouse wrote that he had made 50,000 special bricks for the Wilts & Berks Canal Co. but he had not been able to send them because of low water in the summit level and the Canal Company had to get them from the other end of their system. Cider merchants James Harper & Sons of Ebley wrote that their agent in Swindon had carried cider to Swindon for two-fifths of the railway charge but the last cargo of about 12 tons got bunged up in the summit and had to be carted into the town. County Surveyor Robert Phillips reported that thousands of tons of road stone had been sent round by rail and traction engine to Kempsford, Fairford and Lechlade, costing hundreds of pounds more than carriage by canal.

At this time, the canal was owned by the Great Western Railway Company, who had minimal interest in preserving a decaying route carrying little traffic, however important it was to those involved. So it is not surprising that their Canal Committee announced that from 30th December 1893, the portion of the canal from Bell Lock, Chalford to the Thames would be closed to through traffic until further notice. This immediately

The official closure notice issued by the London office of the Thames & Severn Canal Company in 1893. GA TS/193/13

THAMES & SEVERN CANAL.

Notice is hereby given that on and after the 30th December, 1893, the portion of this Canal, extending from Chalford Chapel Pound at Bell Lock to the junction of the Navigation with the River Thames at Inglesham, and including the Branch Canal from Siddington to Cirencester, will be closed for through traffic, until further notice.

BY ORDER.

J. MAHON,

Clerk to the Company.

Paddington, London, 28th December, 1893.

generated widespread opposition, which led to a series of high level meetings to determine the long term future of the canal. James Smart used his friendship with the Gardiner family of Daneway to ask Lord Bathurst of Cirencester and others to use their influence against closing of the canal. He was also called by those wishing to take over the canal to advise on what needed to be done to get reasonable navigation right through to the Thames and also on the Thames.

Although the canal east of Bell Lock was formally closed and no water was pumped into the summit, boats could still pass when natural supplies made it possible and there was a bonus for the traders as no charges were made for using the 'closed' section. Passage of the summit then became totally dependent on the amount of recent rain. In late February 1894, James Smart's boat carrying deals from Price, Walker & Co. to Reading was held up for three weeks but in the second half of March his boats took good loads of road stone over the summit.

Trouble returned in April, however, when boats belonging to James Smart and others

Bell Lock at Chalford, which became the official terminus of the Thames & Severn Canal in 1893. NP

A distant view of the pumping engine house at Thames Head. NP

A circa 1900 view of the Coates portal at the eastern end of the Sapperton Tunnel. NP

became stuck in the summit pound. The boatmen arranged for one of the pumphouse operators to start up the pump at Smart's expense but the operator was not able to get access. He wrote to Smart: '*I promised your men I would work Saturday night and should have done it but Hewlett simply locked the engine house up and went to Cirencester because I should not work it. I thought I should let you know the reason*'. Smart evidently made other arrangements and in due course the Canal Committee sent him an account for wages, etc, paid in connection with working the steam engine at Thames Head.

One of Smart's boats stuck at the summit was carrying grain for Jacobs & Son of Burford and whilst they were marooned there, Jacobs & Son wrote: '*The delay is a very serious matter, and the grain will be refused if not sent on at once. Please let me know when the boats will arrive*'. A week later, they wrote again: '*When will the boat be at Lechlade Wharf? We have already lost the sale of the barley and must claim on you for loss of profit*'. It seems that another boat stuck belonged to Matthew Hicks of Lechlade, as a letter from Hicks to Smart refers to a contribution towards the expense of pumping: '*… which is I am sure my share, considering the number of boats that were in the summit*'.

Another boat that had evidently been trapped in the summit pound eventually delivered sawdust to Cirencester at the end of April and there loaded a cargo for Lechlade, needing a punt to carry part of the load down the arm to the main canal because of the low water level. Boatman H. Gardner wrote to James Smart: '*We are loaded at last. We have got about 24 tons in and we have been [two days] with the punt getting it down. Please send me one pound by return of post to the GPO Lechlade till called for. Please tell us if the engine is*

going to work any more or not. If there is any water at all, we will try to bring up some gravel to the wharf to make it a bit better'. A few more boats crossed the summit in early May 1894 but then the route was abandoned, although Smart's boats continued to deliver occasional cargoes of coal to Daneway.

The high level discussions that followed the protests about the closure of the Thames & Severn Canal east of Chalford led to a group of canal companies and local authorities forming a Trust which took ownership of the waterway in 1895. After much restoration work, the canal was opened again in 1899, with James Smart's boats carrying many full loads of road stone over the summit in February and right through to Lechlade in March. Some loads of round timber from the Thames Valley were taken west. To publicise the reopening, Smart's boat *Trial* was sent all the way to London, returning on 11th April with 92 bales of colonial wool for mill owner Charles Henry Hooper at Eastington. During the

*James Smart's boat **Trial** at Wallbridge, after returning from a special trip to London in 1899 to mark the reopening of the Thames & Severn Canal. GA D2899*

Work at Blue House near Siddington, part of the major restoration managed by Gloucestershire County Council. WA R1969

summer, however, it soon became apparent that the summit level was still leaking badly and traffic over it ceased again. After more high level discussions, the Thames & Severn Canal was eventually taken over by the County Council in 1901.

Under the auspices of the County Council, great efforts were made to re-open the Thames & Severn Canal through to Lechlade and James Smart was called upon to help occasionally, by providing horses for hauling, and by carrying cement and other materials by boat up to Daneway. Eventually, Smart's ***Providence*** was the first boat over the restored summit in January 1904, carrying coal to the pumping engine at Thames Head and ***Industry*** was the first boat through to Lechlade in March carrying grain. Perhaps hoping this restoration would open up opportunities for business, Smart purchased a newly published guide to waterways all over the country – *Bradshaw's Canals & Navigable Rivers*.

Chapter 13

Away from the Water

By the 1890s, James Smart was well established as the principal carrier operating on the Stroudwater and Thames & Severn canals, in spite of not being able to read or write. From the start, he had been helped by his wife Martha and in later years also by his third son James Henry, known as Harry – his eldest son William Thomas had emigrated to Canada and his second son Frederick Charles ran a grocer's shop in the village. Smart evidently spent much time managing the movement of his boats and barges around the waterways but he was also engaged in activities away from the water that were vital to the success of his whole operation. Surviving letters from the 1880s and '90s refer to topics such as attending markets, arranging vessel maintenance, managing animals, making deliveries by road and managing finance and property.

James Smart in his later years. MM

As well as communicating by letter, James Smart kept in touch with some of his customers by visiting local towns on market day, to which he travelled by pony and trap. Many surviving letters refer to meeting Smart in Gloucester on a Saturday, either at an office or a prominent landmark. Two letters from coal agent Bernard Edwards refer to Smart paying him money and another said that if he missed the eleven o'clock train, he would not be at the office but would be at the Cross by two o'clock. Severn Navigation toll collector George Harris invited Smart to call in at his office to acknowledge receipt of money sent. One letter referred to a discussion with fellow barge owner Hubert Field of Saul and another suggested concluding the sale of a pony at the cattle market at ten o'clock.

Other letters express regret about not meeting Smart. Chepstow stone merchant William Davis could not get to Gloucester the day Smart had asked but hoped to come the following Saturday. Waterman Payne had looked for Smart in Gloucester as he had left his boat and was hoping Smart would employ him. Life insurance agent Sydney Thomas from Coleford said he would write again to say when he would next be at Gloucester on a Saturday. Captain Alfred Meadows at Epney suggested that while Smart was in Gloucester, he could send urgent instructions by carrier John Knight, who could be contacted at the Talbot Inn. Other letters refer to meetings at Stroud Market on a Friday and at Cirencester and Nailsworth markets on a Tuesday.

James Smart's barges and narrowboats needed regular maintanance and this was usually carried out at Matthew Gardiner's yard at The Bourne, near Brimscombe. For an overhaul,

Boats moored beside the boat building and repairing yard at Bourne run by Matthew Gardiner. HB

work done could include replacing planks, repairing a gunwhale, sealing seams with oakum, coating a hull with tar, and sealing and painting cabin woodwork. Accounts also show charges for oiling top cloths, banding and painting a water cask, repairing a windlass, fitting a second-hand rudder and providing tillers, shafts, bowsprits and a second-hand boat's stove. Separate accounts from resident blacksmith Samuel Hewlett included charges for stem plates, keel irons and chimney pipes, and repairs to water pumps, mast box bands and a stove. His total bill was reduced by the value of coal that had been supplied by Smart. For painting the boats, Smart employed Alfred Phillips of Brimscombe, who also worked as a plumber, glazier and paperhanger. When the Bourne yard was busy, Smart did get some maintenance work done by Joseph Gardiner (Matthew's nephew) at Saul.

For new ropes and sails, Smart made use of firms in Gloucester and further afield. Surviving letters refer to ropes supplied by Nurse Brothers and Brimmell & Son of Gloucester and to 50 fathoms of $4^1/_2$ inch cordage hawser, made by Gourock Ropework, Port Glasgow. New sails for *Excelsior* were made by W.J. Newth (late Winfield) of Gloucester. For sail repairs, Smart called on the services of G. Newman & Son at Saul Junction. After *Flora*'s mainsail was blown to pieces in a gale, Captain Meadows wrote from the Junction that Newman thought the sail was worth repairing and was willing to meet Smart at Stroud to discuss it, adding a request for Smart to bring a spare sail for use on the next voyage. For horse harness, Smart dealt with saddler E.N. King of Stonehouse, whilst the Gloucester Iron & Metal Co. supplied hardware such as pulley blocks, lifebuoys and a sack truck.

James Smart also had to spend time making provision for his horses and donkeys, and several surviving letters refer to paying rent for fields or for supplying animal food. Smart received regular supplies of oats and bran from Clark Brothers, corn & cake merchants at neighbouring Chalford Mill and as they used Smart to bring them coal, the cost of the animal food was offset against it. In a similar way, farmers William Whiting of Daneway and George Arnold of Sapperton supplied hay and straw in exchange for coal. Bran was obtained from H. Lambourn, corn meal & flour stores, Wallbridge, and from Henry Cole & Co. Ltd, Cotswold Steam Flour Mills, Lewis Lane, Cirencester. A few letters refer to buying and selling horses and donkeys, including one from coal merchant John Butt of Dudbridge acknowledging a payment of £4 10s for two donkeys.

Although most of the coal carried by Smart's boats and barges was delivered direct to businesses along the line of the Stroudwater and Thames & Severn canals, much was also discharged at his own wharf at Chalford, for supplying small consignments to local customers. Deliveries were made by horse and cart or by donkey and cart around the narrow lanes above Chalford. Surviving letters request coal to be delivered to houses in Chalford, Brownshill, Bussage, France Lynch, Bournes Green, Oakridge, Waterlane, Daneway, Frampton Mansell and even as far as Cherington, Bisley, The Camp and Sheepscombe. Several of these asked for delivery 'as soon as possible', as the writer had nearly run out, and one, again showing remarkable confidence in the postal system, reminded Smart of his promise to deliver that day. Other letters included an apology for not being able to pay for the coal immediately, usually with a promise to settle up soon but one just explained that the writer had been very ill since Christmas and had not earned a penny. One letter was about delivering patent fuel and two postcards asked for coke.

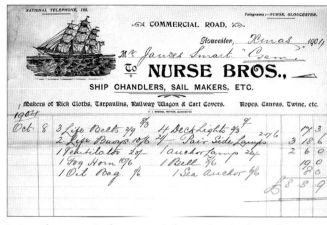

Invoice for equipment needed for James Smart's new barge **Gem** in 1904.
MiP 2008.74/117

Invoice for oats and bran supplied to James Smart in 1898.
GA D4367/2/2 C59

For delivering coal around the narrow lanes on the steep sides of the Chalford Valley, Smart had a small cart that was pulled by a donkey. A zealous policeman noted that the unladen weight was not shown on the cart, nor was the weight of coal shown on the delivery ticket. Harry Smart explained to the magistrates that there was no convenience on Chalford Hill for weighing a cart like this and they often had to deliver a ton in several loads to places on the top of the hill. The chairman said that the defendant had technically broken the law but there was no doubt that their intentions were honest enough and a nominal inclusive fine of 17 shillings would be imposed.

To meet demand in the winter, it seems that the carters worked long hours, as one letter from Miss Clutterbuck of St. Mary's Mill House, Chalford specified that the coal must not come at night. She also asked for it to be put in the coal house without spoiling the gravel. In spite of the long hours, it was difficult at times for Smart to meet all his customers' needs. Charles de Bary of Ashmeads complained that a promised delivery had not arrived, leaving him quite out of coal and he pressed Smart to send some at once. When Mrs Maw's coal did not arrive, she wrote, '*I was without any fire last evening. I had to boil the kettle with wood this morning. Can you send a donkey load early this morning.*' Not being willing to wait for a delivery, widow Livia Newth of Bisley wrote, '*Please don't trouble to send the coal I ordered last week. I am quite out and have had to get some where it will come quicker*'.

As well as distributing coal, surviving letters show that James Smart provided a road delivery service for many other commodities. Retired wine merchant James Newns wanted small quantities of bran delivered to Stroud; Miss C. George asked for oats to be delivered to Cherington Park; Oakridge shopkeeper John Peacey ordered half a ton of salt; James Webb of Rodmarton wanted to know the value of wood he had asked Smart to deliver to Dangerfield's walking stick mill in Chalford; William Selwyn wanted bales of old carpets moved from Brimscombe Wharf to his mill in the Toadsmoor Valley; hay trusser William Beckingham wanted wagons to be available to carry away hay he was cutting; Ernest Simmonds of Minchinhampton asked if Smart could bring up two or three apple trees; and the Cirencester Highway Board wanted road stone hauled from a canal wharf to where it was needed. Smart's wagons also collected two truck loads of Clee Hill road stone from Brimscombe station and made other collections from there on behalf of R.T. Smith & Co., who were the main railway agents for delivering in the Stroud Valley.

Further work for James Smart's horses and wagons involved

Request for James Smart to deliver bales of old carpets to Toadsmoor Mills in 1893. GA D4367/2/2 C25

collecting coal from Brimscombe station, when small quantities of a particular grade were needed urgently or sent as a sample. Surviving letters were mostly from suppliers who normally sent coal by water, such as Park Iron Mines, Dean Forest Navigation, Cannock & Rugeley Collieries and Conduit Collieries. Smart also received coal from Shrewsbury agents A. Boulton & Co., who dealt with Shropshire, Cannock and Leicestershire collieries. Two letters from Forest coal agent Bernard Edwards refer to individual wagons being sent in error and asking Smart if he could unload them. A postcard from Edwards complained that one of his wagons had not been returned nine days after it had reached Brimscombe, adding: *'unless the wagon be returned at once, demurrage will be enforced'*. Smart himself began to make more use of railway transport in the late 1890s, after he hired some private user wagons from the Gloucester Railway Carriage & Wagon Co. and he benefitted from the opening of a station at Chalford in 1897.

Railway wagon purchased from the Gloucester Railway Carriage & Wagon Co. Ltd in June 1924. GA D4791/16/72 No. 4493

Chalford station and goods yard circa 1908, with the Thames & Severn Canal below. The railway began to play an ever more important role in Smart's business from the late 1890s. A Clark Bros horse-drawn covered waggon loads directly from a railway van. NP

Tree trunks beside the road at Daneway waiting to be turned into sawn timber by the saw mill.
HB

As well as the usual carts and wagons used for moving most goods, Smart also had some long timber carriages designed for carrying heavy tree trunks. These were used particularly for hauling timber to the saw mills in the Stroud Valley that had been felled in the woods on the surrounding hills. Smart was known as a shrewd judge of the cubical content of standing trees, which he bought and transported to a mill. Unfortunately, when a wood on the Daneway Estate was being cleared, one carriage was late arriving and this upset Charles Smith, who owned the wood and the Victoria Joinery Works to which the trees were being sent. Smith complained that the wagon only passed his house in Chalford High Street at the time it should have been at Daneway, which meant his men were left standing idle waiting for it, and by the time it was loaded and reached his works, his men had all gone home.

For moving a really big tree, some organisation was needed to ensure all necessary resources were available on site. Messrs King & Scarborough of Ryeford Saw Mills wrote: *'With regard to the large elm at Cirencester, Mr Lock says the butt has about 175 feet cube in it. This we want you to bring. If you have not a carriage strong enough, you can use one of our large ones. The smaller part of the tree contains 80 feet cube to 90 feet cube. This our three horses will bring. Mr Lock's horses will be there on Monday morning next to help load and get out. Please say if you can let us have one horse on Monday as Jilly is lame'.* On one occasion, Smart sent one of his wagons into Wiltshire to haul timber to Swindon.

While a wood at Duntisbourne was being cleared, one of James Smart's timber carriages, pulled by three horses and carrying about five tons, was involved in a serious accident at the top of Cowcombe Hill, leading down to Chalford. When carter Joseph Deane was putting the wheel slide down to act as a brake, he tripped over a ridge in the road and fell under the wheels of the carriage. As the horses and carriage went on down the hill, the heavily laden carriage, soon over-ran the poor animals, and the whole concern went over the bank into an orchard, whereby one horse was killed and another injured. Deane was bandaged on the spot and taken to Stroud hospital but the local newspaper reported that he was not expected to recover. Another Smart employee, Albert Aldridge, also by some means got under the wheels of a timber carriage he was driving and he was lucky only to suffer a broken leg.

James Smart's timber carriages were in the news again after they were blamed for causing obstructions. On the first occasion, two carriages were left outside the Malakoff Inn at Ebley for an hour and the two drivers were fined. On the second occasion, one carriage caused such a blockage in Chalford that, as well as a small fine for the driver, the magistrates also imposed a much larger fine on James Smart himself for permitting the obstruction.

Smart also provided horses when needed for helping other people's heavy wagons up the local hills. In particular, the Cotswold Association, based at the Steam Flour Mill in Lewis Lane, Cirencester, regularly asked for one or two horses to help their wagons up Cowcombe Hill on the road to Cirencester.

As well as all these varied activities to manage, it seems that Smart and his family were good at keeping track of the many financial transactions involved and they were adept at deferring payments when they could. Although Smart did not have a formal credit account with the canal companies, it is apparent from tonnage books that he was always late in paying his canal tolls, compared with other carriers. Also, a number of surviving letters concern suppliers seeking settlement of overdue invoices. In one letter, the Powell, Duffryn Coal Co. pressed for payment of coal supplied four months earlier. Timber merchants John Bland & Co. wanted payment of goods received eight months earlier, whilst sack contractors Halcomb & Co. even hinted at legal action after

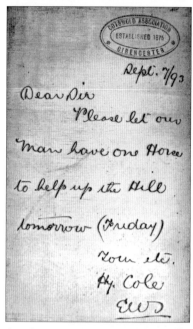

A Cotswold Association postcard. GA D4848

The faded advertisement on the gable end of Smart's house, in 1990. RW

Smart had ignored an earlier invoice for a tarpaulin. Of course, Smart himself also suffered from late payments, such as when Gloucester timber merchant W. Wibby wrote saying he could not pay for goods carried because he had not been paid by a customer. Two weeks later, Wibby sent £40 on account and hoped to send the rest during the following week.

Financial matters became particularly stressful early in 1893, when Stroudwater manager W.J. Snape wrote seeking payment for the last three months tolls and again in April for the last two months. At the same time, the Thames & Severn manager was also pressing for

tonnage payments. Meanwhile, Smart's bank manager asked him to reduce his overdraft from £450 to the agreed limit of £300. Three weeks later, the bank manager wrote again noting that the overdraft was down but still over the limit and he suggested the need for a discussion. During this difficult period, Smart sought relief by deferring payment for a field he was renting but local landowner C.H. Stanton was not sympathtic. He wrote: *'I am sorry you have not had a good year, but these things of course happen in the ordinary course of business. For the rent and tithe rent charge, you can send me a cheque or pay it into the bank as most convenient to yourself'*. Snape wrote four more letters seeking toll payments during the summer but then Smart's difficulties eased and, by the autumn, the frequency of financial letters returned to normal.

A possible contributor to James Smart's cash flow difficulties in early 1893 was that he was in the process of purchasing a property, as referred to in a letter from his solicitors Messrs Little & Mills. His business must have generally been doing well, as he had previously bought two houses at Valley Corner which he rented to tenants. He was also renting land at Nashend Farm from C.H. Stanton and had started a sideline in farming. Later in 1893, Smart bought a small field on the south bank of the River Frome behind the Company's Arms, and three houses and some land at The Frith beyond Oakridge, where he already had some sheep on the land. By 1895, he had bought more land at Oakridge Lynch and a house and land at Bournes Green.

The eastern end of Chalford village, known as Valley Corner, where James Smart owned some houses. HB

Golden Valley at Chalford

Chapter 14

Twentieth Century

B y the early years of the 20th century, James Smart's son James Henry (Harry) Smart was playing an increasing role in the family business, particularly with carrying-by-boat activities. This allowed Smart senior to develop an interest in farming and in his will, written in 1910, he gave his primary occupation as farmer, as well as coal and timber merchant. The family business continued to be profitable and by 1914, Smart had invested in more houses in Chalford and Chalford Hill, and in land at Ashmeads and Chalford Hill. Also, Harry Smart owned his own house at Randalls Green. The business was sometimes referred to as Smart & Son but the formal name on notepaper remained in the name of James Smart alone and surviving documents do not usually allow the roles of the two men to be differentiated. In the following account, therefore, it should be understood that the name Smart could be a reference to father, to son or to both.

Harry Smart in his later years. MM

At the beginning of the new century, Smart's main barge was *Onward*, which regularly collected road stone from Chepstow for the various highway authorities along the Stroud Valley. On the outward journey, she occasionally carried gravel from Dudbridge to Bristol and she also made occasional trips to Newport, to load manganese ore for paint manufacturers S.G. Bailey & Co. at Stafford Mill. As it was difficult to discharge a large barge at this mill, it was usual to transfer half the cargo into a narrowboat at Saul Junction and then to unload this once *Onward* was empty. Smart's other barge *Perseverance* mainly carried Forest coal from the Sharpness tip and some road stone from Chepstow to various places along the Stroud Valley. When at Stroud one day, her captain Henry Ralph let his pair of donkeys wander on to the highway and when taken before the magistrates, he was fined 5 shillings.

In 1901, Smart had a new barge built by Matthew Gardiner at the Bourne yard named *Temperance*. She had the usual open hold, flat bottom and single mast of Smart's other barges but when she was first taken down the canal, she became stuck under a bridge, because her bulwarks were higher than usual to give better protection when out in the estuary. Once *Temperance* was in service, *Onward* was sold. The new barge's main role was to continue the Chepstow stone trade, and surviving invoices from stone merchant William Davis show that she usually loaded 85 tons of rough stone, lifts or broken stone but as the depth of water in the canal would only allow her to carry 70 tons, the excess had to be left at Whitminster Lock to be collected later. *Temperance* also made occasional trips to

*James Smart's boat **Trial**
at Dudbridge Wharf,
circa 1907. NH2*

Cardiff to collect coal for John Francillon of Gloucester, who ran the passenger steamers on the Sharpness Canal, and she made one trip to Newport in 1902 to collect manganese ore for S.G. Bailey & Co. In 1904, Smart had another barge, **Gem**, built at the Bourne yard and **Temperance** was sold.

Smart's narrowboats continued to collect coal from the Midlands and from the tip at Sharpness, with some going through to Valley Corner at Chalford, where cousin William Smart had a coal yard. Surviving letters show that Smart was also receiving coal by rail to Chalford station from the Forest of Dean and from Conduit Colliery, Norton Canes, both previously served by boats. Much road stone was collected from Saul Junction, where schooners from Arklow and steamers from Penmaenmawr off-loaded direct into Smart's boats and barges. The reverse operation was carried out in 1904, when 140 tons of manganese ore was taken from Stafford Mill to the Junction to be loaded on to the ketch **Beatrice Hannah**, destined for Dublin. Two unusual cargoes in 1904 were 15 tons of machinery carried from Haywood, Lancashire to Ham Mill and a reaping machine carried from Stonehouse to Chalford. One of Smart's captains had a shock when he returned to his boat at Stroud one morning and found an intruder had broken into the cabin. When the intruder refused to leave, he was arrested and as he had broken in, he was sentenced to 14 days hard labour.

Following the restoration of the Thames & Severn Canal, Smart's boats were once again able to carry grain, fertilizer, bricks and road stone to Cirencester, Kempsford and Lechlade, returning with gravel from Cerney Wick and round timber from Cirencester. However, as the North Wilts and Wilts & Berks canals were in a poor state, the former timber traffic from Wiltshire and the Thames Valley did not return. Also, the traffic that did return was subject to interruption, as some of the restoration work had not been up to standard. As a result, the canal had to be closed for repairs from time to time to reduce leakages and this also inhibited new traffic. Following an approach from the managers of the borax factory at Inchbrook in the Nailsworth Valley, four of Smart's boats took 78 tons of the mineral boracite from Dudbridge to London for their main factory, with high hopes of much more to come. However, as the load a boat could carry over the summit was limited, only two more consignments went via the Thames & Severn Canal, while four others were sent all of the way round via the Midlands. To make matters worse, the Great Western Railway then reduced their rate to London for boracite by 5s per ton.

As repeated repairs failed to make the Thames & Severn Canal watertight and with only a modest income from tolls, the County Council were forced to consider whether it was worth continuing to pump water into the summit. James Smart tried to keep traffic moving and three of his boats did each carry 24 tons of fertilizer through the tunnel in April 1911 but

Cerney Wick Lock, near where gravel was loaded by the last boat through Sapperton Tunnel in 1911. NP

due to the usual seasonal drop in water level, the matter soon came to a head. On 11th May, Smart's boat *Gem* passed through the tunnel with 20 tons of stone intended to improve the roadway over Dudgrove Bridge. On the way back, *Gem* carried 20 tons of gravel from Cerney Wick to Cirencester and there loaded 1 ton of round timber. Captain George Gleed later told how, even with that light cargo, they could not get through the tunnel, and they had to go and get someone to start the pump specially for them. They eventually passed through on 23rd May 1911, in the process becoming the last trading boat to cross the summit.

Meanwhile, James Smart's barge *Gem* (not to be confused with his narrowboat of the same name) was still making regular trips to Chepstow to collect road stone but this was about to change. The demand for Chepstow stone was reducing because road authorities preferred a harder stone and so *Gem* was taken out of service by the end of 1911, leaving *Perseverance* to handle the remaining work. Four years later, Smart's Chepstow contracts dried up and he was left with no further work in the estuary.

James Smart's **Gem** at the Bourne yard, painted by Edith Ferrabee. MiP 1974.187. PP

The First World War made life difficult for Smart's business, as many of his employees joined the armed forces. By July 1917, there was much concern in Chalford about coal supplies for the following winter. Writing to P.G. Snape, who had taken over from his father as Stroudwater Canal manager, Harry Smart wrote: '*I still have two of my boats tied up for lack of men. I applied to the War Office direct last August, stating my position fully, asking for WC Gardiner, one of my old captains over 42 years of age, then ill in France. Then my next [target]* was Ernest Franklin. After [his] boat had been tied up ten weeks, he returned'. What boats Smart did have available were kept busy carrying Forest coal from the Sharpness tip to the mills along the Stroud Valley, together with some domestic coal to Chalford. When news of the armistice eventually reached the village, a cannon was fired from Smart's coal wharf, the sound of which together with the ringing of the church bells helped to spread the good news to the villages and hamlets on the tops of the hills.

After the war, Smart's boatmen returned but trading conditions continued to deteriorate due to railway competition and poor canal maintenance. In 1921, Smart joined with fellow carrier E.T. Ward & Son of Stroud in pressing for a reduction in tolls on the Stroudwater Navigation and this was agreed but the condition of the Thames & Severn Canal remained a problem. In 1922, Smart claimed £9 from the Thames & Severn Committee for detention of boats at Chalford due to the lock gates and paddles not being in good order. He refused an offer of £3 3s and accepted £4. Later that year, Smart's boat *Trial* became stuck in Bowbridge Lock because there was not enough water in the pound above to get over the top cill. The following morning, the boatmen had to walk up beyond Brimscombe, opening sluices, to get enough water to move on. Smart blamed the lockkeepers for not having ensured that the lock gates were closed properly after a previous boat had passed through.

To try to highlight the poor condition of the Thames & Severn Canal, Smart arranged for his barge *Perseverance* to carry a full load of 50 tons of coal from Stroud to Brimscombe on 4th January 1923, instead of the part load that it normally carried because of a lack of dredging. The barge was hauled by two donkeys and at times several men assisted on the line. A large quantity of water had to be passed down from the upper reaches of the canal as the barge was dragging the bottom all the way and the journey of about two miles took 3 hours 40 minutes. The Chairman of the Stroudwater Company then wrote to the County Council complaining that they were not maintaining the canal properly and, as the waterway was so narrowed by mud, it was now impossible to work it to commercial advantage. However, the Council's Canal Committee considered that as the canal was sufficient to accept boats which generally used it (mostly carrying about 30 tons), they were quite unable to recommend any dredging to accommodate larger barges.

While these exchanges about the condition of the Thames & Severn Canal were taking place, a more serious incident stopped the traffic completely on the Stroudwater Canal. On 4th January 1923, while Smart's boat *Trial* was rising in the Bristol Road Lock, the bottom gates were struck by the motor boat *Alfreda*, which was towing another boat, both laden with coal. The impact was sufficient to smash the gates, allowing the resultant rush of water from the lock to carry both boats downstream. The crews emerged unscathed but the local newspaper reported that the experience of Smart's boatmen was '*an exciting one*'. The canal remained closed for two months and Smart tried to claim for loss of business but the Canal Company repudiated liability.

Bristol Road Bridge with the gates of the adjoining lock visible through the arch. GA K185/1, 1948

After a long and successful life, James Smart senior died on 3rd April 1923, aged 83. He had come from working as a teenage bread-winner for his poor family to being the leading carrier on the Stroud Valley canals, in spite of not being able to read or write. He was a regular attender at the Chalford Tabernacle, a life-long teetotaller, a non-smoker and a strong Liberal in politics. In developing his business, he had been much helped by his wife, Martha Ann, who had died six years earlier. After this, the business became known as J.H. Smart & Sons.

During the 1920s, Harry Smart struggled to keep the waterways business going, mainly carrying coal from the Sharpness tip to Brimscombe and from Cannock Chase to Chalford

The hulk of James Smart's barge **Perseverance** abandoned on the bank at Ryeford. NMM

J.H. Smart & Sons lorry. MM

but vessel movements became increasingly difficult. Boatman Ernie Franklin later remembered: *'In June and July, there was a weed in the canal called fennel. Then it took us much longer to come up the canal, because as you moved, the fennel did roll up in rolls and this stopped the boat. One had to be on the fore end with a shaft to fork it away from the bow of the boat. I left Stroud at 4.30 in the morning, and I didn't get to Chalford until six o'clock at night – I thought this is too bad'*. As the traffic diminished, the County Council began to think about closing the Thames & Severn Canal and with no prospect of any improvement in maintenance, Harry Smart decided to give up his remaining boat **Providence** and barge **Perseverance** in 1930.

The last recorded trip of barge **Perseverance** was taking a load of coal from Brimscombe to Ebley in September 1930 and then she was abandoned in Wallbridge Basin. Five years later, the Stroudwater Committee asked Smart to move her or the usual charges would be made, so he arranged for her to be hauled out of the water on to a field to the west of the Anchor Inn at Ryeford. While there, her lines were recorded by enthusiasts, who recognised she was one of the last complete examples of what became called a Stroud barge, narrow enough to pass the locks of both the Stroudwater and Thames & Severn canals. Unfortunately, she did not stay complete for long as parts were taken by local people for hen enclosures, firewood and the like, and the remains were eventually burned.

Although J.H. Smart & Sons stopped moving coal by water, they continued to act as coal merchants and hauliers, bringing in coal by rail and motor lorry. When Harry Smart died in 1945, the business was continued by his surviving son Raymond James and then sold to outsiders. In the 1970s, the business moved away from Chalford but the trading name was retained into the early years of the 21st century.

Index